The History of the Devils of Loudun

The History of the Devils of Loudun
After the Original Report of 1634
Translator and editor: Edmund Goldschmid

Original title: *La Veritable Histoire des Diables de Loudun, de la possession des Religieuses Ursulines et de la Condamnation d'Urbain Grandier, par un temoin (1634)*
Cover image: illustration from the book *La Religieuse* by *Martin van Maele*
Lay-out: www.burokd.nl

ISBN 978-94-92355-25-6

© 2017 Revised publication by:

VAMzzz Publishing
P.O. Box 3340
1001 AC Amsterdam
The Netherlands
www.vamzzz.com
contactvamzzz@gmail.com

THE HISTORY OF
THE DEVILS OF
LOUDUN

After the Original Report of 1634

Translated and edited by

Edmund Goldschmid

VAMzzz PUBLISHING

LA VERITABLE HISTOIRE

DES

𝔇𝔦𝔞𝔟𝔩𝔢𝔰 𝔡𝔢 𝔏𝔬𝔲𝔡𝔲𝔫,

De la possession des Religieuses

Ursulines

et

de la Condamnation

D'URBAIN GRANDIER,

Par UN TEMOIN.

A. POITIERS,
Chez J. Thoreau et la veuve Ménier,
Imprimeurs ordinaires du Roi
et de l'Universitié.

M. D C. X X X I V.

Urbain Grandier
Bouère 1590 – 18 August 1634, Loudun

contents

Post Scriptum

Introduction

THE FOLLOWING EXTRAORDINARY account of the "*Cause Célè-bre*" of Urbain Grandier, the *Curé* of Loudun, accused of Magic and of having caused the Nuns of the Convent of Saint Ursula to be possessed of devils, is written by an eye-witness, and not only an eye-witness but an actor in the scenes he describes. It is printed at "*Poitiers, chez J. Thoreau et la veuve Ménier, Imprimeurs du Roi et de l'Université, 1634.*" I believe two copies only are known: my own, and the one in the National Library, Paris. The writer is Monsieur des Niau, Counsellor at la Flèche, evidently a firm believer in the absurd charges brought against Grandier.

Magic appears to have had its origin on the plains of Assyria, and the worship of the stars was the creed of those pastoral tribes who, pouring down from the mountains of Kurdistan into the wide level where Babylon afterwards raised its thousand towers, founded the sacerdotal race of the *Chasdim* or *Chaldeans*. To these men were soon alloted peculiar privileges and ascribed peculiar attributes, until, under the name of Magi, they acquired a vast and permanent influence. Their temples were astronomical observatories as well as holy places; and the legendary tower of Babel, in the Book of Genesis, is probably but the mythical equivalent of a vast edifice consecrated to the study of the seven planets, or perhaps, as the *Bab* (court or palace) of *Bel*, to the brilliant star of good fortune alone. Availing themselves of the general adoration of the stars, they appear to have invented a system of astrology—the apotelesmatic science—by which they professed to decide upon the nature of coming events and the complexion of individual fortunes, with especial reference to the planetary aspects.

In Persia magic assumed a yet more definite development. The Chaldeans had attributed the origin of all things to a great central everlasting fire. The foundation of the Persian system, usually ascribed to Zerdusht or Zoroaster, was the existence of two antagonistic principles—Ormuzd, the principle of good, and Ahriman, the principle of evil. In Persia everything associated with science or religion was included under the denomination "magic." The Persian priests were named the Magnise or Magi, but they did not arrogate to themselves the entire credit of intercourse with the gods. Zoroaster, who was King of Bactria, made some reservations for the sake of exalting the regal power, and taught that the kings were illuminated by a celestial fire which emanated from Ormuzd. Hence the sacred fire always preceded the monarch as a symbol of his illustrious rank; and Plato says the Persian kings studied magic, which is a worship of their gods.

It was, however, in Egypt, that magic received its development as an art. The most famous temples in Egypt were those of Isis, at

Memphis and Busiris; of Serapis, at Canopus, Alexandria, and Thebes; of Osiris, of Apis, and Phtha. Isis, the wife of Osiris, derives her name from the Coptic word *isi*, or plenty, and would seem to typify the earth; but she is usually represented as the goddess of the moon (Gr. *kerasphôros*, the horn-bearing). Isis was also employed as a personification of wisdom, and to a certain extent she may be regarded as a symbol of the eternal will, her shrines bearing the enigmatic inscription—"I am the all that was, that is, that will be; no mortal can raise my veil." Horus was the son of Isis, and was instructed by his mother in the art of healing. Horus, synonymous with light, is the king or spirit of the sun. Astrological science and magic were earnestly and eagerly studied by the Egyptian priests. It was their belief that the different stars exercised a powerful influence on the human body. Their funeral ceremonies may be quoted as an illustration, for they agree in sharing among the divinities the entire body of the dead. To Ra, or the Sun, they assigned the head; to Anubis, the nose and lips; to Hathor, the eyes; to Selk, the teeth; and so on. To ascertain the nativity the astrologer had only to combine the theory of the influences thus exercised by these star-related gods with the aspect of the heavens at the moment of an individual's birth. It was an element of the Egyptian as well as of the Persian astrological doctrine that a particular star controlled the natal hour of everyone.[1]

Through the instrumentality of Orpheus, Musæus, Pythagoras, and others, who had travelled in Egypt, and been initiated by the priests into their mysteries, magic found its way into Greece, and there assumed various novel developments. The Greek sorcery was chiefly manifested in the peculiar rites of the Orpheotelesta, the invocation of the dead, the cave of Trophônios, the oracles of the gods, and the worship of Hekatê. The latter mysterious deity, the moon-goddess, was the patron divinity of the sorcerers. From her, as from one of the powers of the nether world, proceeded phantoms that taught witchcraft, hovered among the tombs, and haunted crossways and places accursed by the blood of the murdered or the suicide. "The Mormô, the Cereops, the Empusa, were among the goblin crew that did her bidding."

Rome borrowed her magic, no less than her art and literature, from poetic Hellas. The occult science does not appear to have been known to the Romans until about 200 years before the Christian era. But they had previously cultivated a modification of the Etruscan sorcery, comprising the divination of the future, the worship of the dead, the evocation of their *lemures* or phantoms, and the mystic ceremonies of the Mana-Genita, a nocturnal goddess of awful character. Numa was the great teacher of the ancient Roman magic, which probably partook both of a religious and medical character.

The Christian church, at the outset of its history, forbade the practice of pagan magic, but taught what may be described as a magic of its own. Both Origen and Tertullian held that mania and epilepsy were produced by the action of demons or evil spirits confined within the bodies of the sufferers, and that these were to be exorcised by certain forms of words. The church formally recognized the efficacy of exorcism in 367, when the Council of Laodicea ordained that only those should practise it who were duly authorized by the bishops. Connected with magic and magical rites were the supposed curative properties of the relics of saints, and the divine origin popularly ascribed to visions and ecstatic trances.

In the middle ages magic asserted its supremacy over the whole of Christian Europe; but it had entirely lost the religious character communicated to it by the Chaldeans. It had degenerated into the "black art." It dealt only with the night-side of nature, with the Evil One and his imps, with the loathsome practises of witchcraft and the enchantments of the necromancer. The scholar rose superior to this low kind of theurgy, but he, too, no longer sought communion with the heavenly powers; he devoted all his energies to the discovery of the philosopher's stone and the elixir of eternal youth, to the sources of illimitable wealth and endless life. [*Encyc. Nat.* ix. p. 52].

Born at Rouvère, near Sablé, at the very end of the sixteenth century, Urbain Grandier was curate and Canon of Loudun. On obtaining this living, he became so popular a preacher that the envy of the monks was excited against him. He was first accused of incontinency; but, being acquitted, his enemies instigated some nuns to play the part of persons possessed, and in their convulsions to charge Grandier with being the cause of their visitation. This horrible, though absurd, charge was countenanced by Cardinal Richelieu, who had been persuaded that Grandier had satirized him. It is this celebrated case which our credulous author here endeavours to prove.

The reader will, no doubt, be interested in the wonderful effects said to have been produced by exorcism. This word is a term applied to the act of driving an evil spirit out of one possessed, by a command in the name of some divine power. The ability to effect this by such means has been accepted as a belief by pagans, Jews, and Christians, and ceremonials with this object are still in use among the Roman Catholics and the closer followers of the teachings of Luther, who continued to keep his opinions in this respect after the Reformation. One of the minor orders of the Roman Catholic clergy exercise the function, and it is only used in cases of supposed demoniacal possession, in the administration of baptism, and in the blessing of the holy oil or *chrism*, and of holy water. [*Nat. Encyc.* v., p. 389].

"Is not my word like as a fire? saith the Lord; and like a hammer that breaketh the rock in pieces?" (Jer. xxiii. 29).

"Healing by words, that is by the direct expression of the mental power," says Van Helmont, "was common in the early ages, particularly in the church, and not only used against the devil and magic arts, but also against all diseases. As it commenced in Christ, so will it continue for ever." (Operatio sanandi a primordio fuit in ecclesia per verba, ritus, exorcismos, aquam, panem, salem, herbas, idque nedum contra diabolos et effectus magicos, sed et morbos omnes. *Opera omnia, de virtute magna verborum et rerum*, p. 753). Not only did the early Christians heal by words, but the old magicians performed their wonders by magic formulas. "Many cures," says the Zendavesta, "are performed by herbs and trees, others by water, and again others by words: for it is by means of the divine word that the sick are the most surely healed." The Egyptians also believed in the magic power of words. Plotin cured Porphyrius, who lay dangerously ill in Sicily, by wonder-working words; and the latter healed the sick by words, and cast out the devil by exorcism. The Greeks were also well acquainted with the power of words, and give frequent testimony of this knowledge in their poems; in the oracles, exhortation and prayer were universal. Orpheus calmed the storm by his song; and Ulysses stopped the bleeding of wounds by the use of certain words. Among the Greeks, healing by words was so common that in Athens it was strictly forbidden. A woman was even stoned for using them, as they said that the gods had given healing virtues to stones, plants, and animals, but not to words (Leonard. Varius de fascino, Paris, 1587, lib. ii. p. 147). Cato is said to have cured sprains by certain words. According to Pliny, he did not alone use the barbaric words "motas, daries, dardaries, astaries," but also a green branch, four or five feet long, which he split in two, and caused to be held over the injured limb by two men. Marcus Varro, it is said, cured tumours by words. Servilius Novianus cured affections of the eyes by causing an inscription to be worn suspended round the neck, consisting of the letters A and Z; but the greatest celebrity was gained by Serenus Sammonicus by his wonder-working hieroglyphics. They were supposed to be a certain cure for fever, and were in the subjoined form:—

ABRACADABRA
BRACADABR
RACADAB
ACADA
CAD
A

Talismans were inscribed with various signs; and many customs still in use in the East originate from them. Angerius Fererius, in his "Vera medendi methodus, lib. ii. c. ii. de homerica medicatione," speaks very plainly on this subject: "Songs and characters have not alone this power: it exists also in a believing mind, which is produced in the unlearned by the help of visible signs, and in the learned by an acknowledged and peculiar influence."

(Non sunt carmina, non characteres, qui talia possunt, sed vis animi confidentis, et cum patiente concordis, ut doctissime a poeta dictum sit:

Nos habitat, non Tartara, sed nec sidera cœli;

Spiritus in nobis qui viget, illa facit.

Doctis et rerum intelligentiam habentibus, nihil opus est externis, sed cognita vi animi, per eam miracula edere possunt. Indoctus ergo animus, hoc est, suæ potestatis et naturæ inscius, per externa illa confirmatus, morbos curare poterit. Doctus vero et sibi constans, solo verbo sanabit; aut ut simul intactum animum afficiat, externa quoque assumet.)

The living Word, which illuminated mankind through Christ, showed its divine power over disease; and the true followers of Christ can perform wonders by the power of his word. "Etenim sanatio in Christo Domino incœpit," says Helmont, "per apostolos continuavit et modo est, atque perennis permanet."—Our Lord said to the sick man, Arise and walk; and he arose and went his way: open thine eyes; and he saw: take up thy bed and walk; and he stood up;

Lazarus, come forth! and he that was dead came forth, bound hand and foot with grave-clothes, and his face was bound about with a napkin, &c. But what is this word, which is sharper than a two-edged sword? It is the Divine spirit, which is ever present, ever active; it is the Divine breath which inspires man. In all ages, and in every nation, there have been men who possessed miraculous powers; but they were inspired by religion—turned towards God in prayer and unity. The Almighty sees the heart of the supplicant, and not alone their words; he sees the belief and intention, and not the rank or education.

Even the pious heathens prayed to God; and their peculiar worship maintained the connection, and brought about a still closer union, between individuals and God, and enabled them, in some measure, to pierce the veil of ignorance and darkness. And the pious heathen endeavoured with all his energies to raise himself to a more intimate relation with God, and, therefore, a peculiar force lay in the means employed; and what could be more powerful than prayer? and God, in his comprehensive love and affection, would not leave these supplicants unanswered.

It would be superfluous to enumerate many instances of the efficacy of prayer, as exemplified in pious and believing men, which we might meet with in all ages, and among all nations. In later times many are well known. I shall, however, mention one, which appears to me the clearest and least doubtful. Kiersen relates as follows: "I knew a seer who gained a power of foretelling the future by prayer during the night on a mountain, where he was accustomed to lie on his face; and he used this power for the assistance of the sick in the most unpretending manner. His visions are partly prosaic, partly poetical, and have reference not only to sickness, but also to other important, and even political, events, so that he has much resemblance to the prophets of the Old Testament."

For those to whom the universe is a piece of clockwork, or a perpetual motion, which continues moving for ever of its own accord—to whom the everlasting power and wisdom and love in eternity and nature is as nothing, prayer and supplication must seem objectless and insipid; but they will never be able to perform the works of the soul. To these, the magical effects are just as inexplicable (and, therefore, untrue) as the magical phenomena are unknown. But, with all their knowledge and wisdom of the world, nature will ever remain to them a mystery.

This is not the place to enter more fully into this subject; but it may not be superfluous to remember that in every word there is a magical influence, and that each word is in itself the breath of the internal and moving spirit. A word of love, of comfort, of promise, is able to strengthen the timid, the weak, or the physically ill; but words of hatred, censure, enmity, or menace, lower our confidence and self-reliance. How easily the worldling, who rejoices under good fortune, is cast down under adversity, and despair only enters where religion is not—where the mind has no inward and divine comforter. But there is, probably, no one who is proof against curse or blessing. [*Ennemoser, Hist. of Magic*, l., p. 120.]

FOOTNOTE:

1.   To those interested in the study of occult science, the publications and reprints issued by Mr. R. Fryar, of Bath, must prove most interesting. As regards Egyptian magic, especially the artistic reproduction of the celebrated Isiac Tablet, with the learned essay thereon, by Mr. W. Wynn Westcott, is invaluable. Happy is the collector who has secured a copy, however, as the edition, like all Mr. Fryar's, is very limited, only 100 copies being printed.

PART I

AT THE BEGINNING of the 17th century, the curate of Loudun was Urbain Grandier. To those talents which lead to success in this world, this man united a corruption of morals which dishonoured his character. His conduct had made him many enemies. These were not merely rivals, but husbands and fathers, some of high position, who were outraged at the dishonour he brought on their family. He was, nevertheless, a wonderfully proud man, and the bitterness of his tongue and the harshness with which he pursued his advantages only excited them the more. And these advantages were numerous, for he had a marvelous faculty for pettifogging. His iniquities had rendered him the scourge of the town, whose principal curate and greatest scandal he was at one and the same moment. This is proved by the dispensations obtained by many fathers of families to assist at the divine service in some other parish, and by the permissions granted them to receive the sacrament from some other hand.[2]

But what was still more serious is, that while setting so many people against him, he had been able to form as formidable a party of his own. These were almost all Huguenots,[3] of which Loudun was then full. He had gained their good graces so much that they upheld him to the utmost of their power. This gave rise to the suspicion that he was merely a disguised Calvinist; a by no means unusual occurrence. Thus Grandier, believing himself safe, put no bounds to his audacity. He treated those from whom he differed with contempt, and in his preachings even dared to question the privileges of the Carmelites. He publicly ridiculed their sermons. He even encroached on episcopal jurisdiction, by granting dispensations from the publication of marriage banns. This last act caused a sensation, and was reported to Louis de la Rocheposay, Bishop of Poitiers, to whom, at the same time, were addressed numerous complaints of the irregular conduct of the curate and of the scandal he caused. The prelate had him arrested, and imprisoned till his trial, which took place on the 2nd June 1630, when he was condemned to fast on bread and water every Friday for three months, forbidden to officiate in the diocese for five years, and interdicted for all time from performing divine service in the town of Loudun. Grandier appealed against this sentence to the Metropolitan, M. d'Escoubleau de Sourdis, Archbishop of Bordeaux, and since then created Cardinal; and the prosecution appealed to the parliament of Paris against this attempt to evade the jurisdiction of the Bishop. But as many witnesses had to be heard, most of whom lived in the diocese, the parliament remitted the case to the Courts of Poitiers. Grandier was thus enabled to face his adversaries, thanks to the friends he had in the district. The following fact proves this.

Amongst other witnesses, two priests, Gervais Méchin, and Louis Boulieau deposed that they had found Grandier lying with women and girls flat on the ground in his Church, the gates leading to the street being shut; that several times, at extraordinary hours, both during the day and during the night they had seen women and girls come to his room; that some remained there from one o'clock in the afternoon, till past midnight, and had their suppers brought there by their maidservants; who used to withdraw at once; that they had also seen him in his Church, with the doors wide open, and, that some women having entered, they were at once closed.

Such evidence was absolute ruin to Grandier; consequently his friends moved heaven and earth. They used bribery and threats against these priests, and obtained from them a retractation of their evidence. René Grandier, brother of the accused, wrote it with his own hand, as was afterwards proved, and the two priests signed it. This evidence destroyed, the cabal had little trouble in turning the legal proceedings to the advantage of Grandier. The Court of Poitiers pronounced his acquittal of the charges brought against him. He was so triumphant, that he insulted his enemies and treated them with public contempt, as if he were entirely 'out of the wood.' He had yet to appear before the tribunal of the Archbishop of Bordeaux, to whom he had appealed. But here again his friends stood by him, and he obtained a second acquittal and an order reinstating him in all his functions (22nd Nov. 1631). The verdict contained a warning to him "to behave well and decently, according to the Holy Decretals and Canonical Constitutions."

At the same time, the Archbishop, in view of the animosity of his adversaries, thought it would be better and safer for him to exchange livings; and he advised him to leave a town where he was looked upon with such disfavour.

Grandier did not think proper to follow the advice or obey the order: far from showing the modesty which was enjoined him, he looked upon his acquittal as a triumph, and returned to Loudun with a laurel branch in his hand, for the mere purpose of insulting his opponents.

Neutral persons were shocked at so little modesty of conduct, his enemies were irritated, and even his friends blamed him. Without pausing an instant he set to work to obtain every advantage over his adversaries. He was not satisfied with having obtained the full mead he was entitled to; he resolved to carry his vengeance as far as law would allow him; and prepared to prosecute before the Courts all those who had taken steps against him, and to claim damages of various amounts, and the restitution of the revenues of his cure, the sentence of the Archbishop of Bordeaux entitling him thereto. In vain did his best friends use every means to turn him from so imprudent a design: God, who intended to cut off this gangrenous member from the body of His Church, and to make of him an example memorable to all ages, abandoned him to his own wilful blindness. Nevertheless, amidst all these proceedings, nothing had been as yet heard of Magic, and up to this time no one had even thought of suspecting him of that crime.

Six years previously, a convent of nuns of the order of St. Ursula had established itself at Loudun. This community, like every new institution, was in somewhat straitened circumstances; though the social position of its members was good. Most of them were daughters of the nobility, while the remainder belonged to the best

"Bourgeoisie" of the country. The good reputation of the new order (it was not quite fifty years old), and the high character it bore in Loudun, had also attracted to it a great number of pupils. The nuns were therefore enabled, with economy, to make ends meet, and could look forward to the future with confidence.

The Mother Superior, Madame de Belfiel, daughter of the Marquis de Cose, was related to M. de Laubardemont, Counsellor of State and afterwards Intendent of the provinces of Touraine, Anjou, and Maine. Madame de Sazilli was a connection of the Cardinal de Richelieu. The two ladies de Barbesiers, sisters, belonged to the house of Nogeret. Madame de la Mothe was daughter of the Marquis de la Motte Baracé in Anjou. There was also a Madame d'Escoubleau, of the same name and family as the Archbishop of Bordeaux. Thus they could flatter themselves with dreams of future successes, when they happened to lose their Prior Moussaut, who had charge of their spiritual welfare.

A successor had now to be sought. Grandier, who had never had any connection with the convent, offered himself nevertheless as a candidate. The proposal was scornfully rejected; and the Superior, Madame de Belfiel, had a great quarrel with one of her friends, who urged her to appoint this priest. The choice of the convent fell on Canon Mignon, a man of considerable merit, and in whom spiritual gifts were only equalled by intellectual ones. Grandier, already irritated at his own want of success, was still more annoyed at Mignon's appointment. The contrast in all points between his character and that of the Canon was too great for any other result to have been looked for. Every honest man takes a pride in the blamelessness of his profession, and cannot look favourably on a colleague who dishonours it, nor speak favourably of him. The curate, then, had nothing to expect from the Canon, who was very intimate with the Bishop,[4] and he had already been made aware of the opinions Mignon had expressed at the time of the first trial. These circumstances were not likely to induce Grandier to look with a kindly eye on his successful competitor, and he consequently determined to give plenty of work to the confessor and to his penitents.

Of the various functions the priest is called upon to perform, none requires such delicacy of treatment as the ministry of the tribunal of Penitence.[5] It becomes still more delicate where the consciences of nuns are concerned. But the burden is intolerable, and few could bear it, if extraordinary agencies are employed to increase the difficulty. The anxiety of a newly-appointed confessor in such a situation would be easily understood by Grandier, and would tend to console him for his failure in obtaining the coveted position.

However this may be, extraordinary symptoms began to declare themselves within the convent, but they were hushed up as far as possible, and not allowed to be known outside the walls. To do otherwise would have been to give the new institution a severe blow, and to risk ruining it at its birth. This the nuns and their confessor understood. It was therefore decided to work in the greatest secrecy, and to cure, or at least mitigate, the evil.

It was hoped that God, touched by the patience with which the chastisement was borne, would Himself, in His mercy, send a remedy.

This was all that prudence could devise, but *human* prudence, always infinitely limited in its views; *Divine* prudence is quite another thing. God had resolved that the mystery of iniquity should no longer lie buried. As the church, at its birth, gained great credit through similar events,[6] so again, in this case, did they serve to revive the faith of true believers, and so it will be again in future times.

Loudun was fated to behold events of this nature, and they were to produce their ordinary effect, viz., to enlighten those whose consciences, though distorted, had preserved some remnants of original good, and to blind souls darkened with pride, and hearts full of perversity.

As usually happens, the extraordinary phenonomena displayed in the persons of the nuns were taken for the effects of sexual disease. But soon suspicions arose that they proceeded from supernatural causes; and at last they perceived what God intended every one to see.

Thus the nuns, after having employed the physicians of the body, apothecaries and medical men, were obliged to have recourse to the physicians of the soul, and to call in both lay and clerical doctors, their confessor no longer being equal to the immensity of the labour. For they were seventeen in number; and everyone was found to be either fully possessed, or partially under the influence of the Evil One.

All this could not take place without some rumours spreading abroad; vague suspicions floated through the city; had the secret even been kept by the nuns, their small means would soon have been exhausted by the extraordinary expenses they were put to in trying to hide their affliction, and this, together with the number of people employed in relieving them, must have made the matter more or less public. But their trials were soon increased when the public was at last made acquainted with their state. The fact that they were possessed of devils drove everyone from their convent as from a diabolical residence, or as if their misfortune involved their abandonment by God and man. Even those who acted thus were their best friends. Others looked upon these women as mad, and upon those who tended them as visionaries. For, in the beginning, people being still calm, had not come to accuse them of being imposters.

Their pupils were first taken from them; most of their relations discarded them; and they found themselves in the deepest poverty. Amidst the most horrible vexations of the invisible spirit, they were forced to labour with their hands, to earn their bread. What was most admirable was that the rule of the community was never broken. Never were they known to discontinue their religious observances, nor was divine service ever interrupted. Ever united, they retained unbroken the bonds of charity which bound them together. Their courage never failed, and when the seizure was past, they used to return to their work or attend the services of the Church with the same modesty and calmness as in the happy days of yore. I know that malice will not be pleased at such a pleasing portraiture. But this base feeling, too natural in the human heart, should be banished thence by all men of honour, who know its injustice and only require that history should be truthful. Probability itself is in favour of our statements. For when God permits us to be attacked so violently by our common enemy, it is as a trial to ourselves, to sanctify us and raise us to a high degree of perfection, and simultaneously He prepares us for victory, and grants us extraordinary grace, which we have only to assimilate and profit by.

It became necessary to have recourse to exorcisms. This word alone is for some people a subject of ridicule, as if it had been clearly proved that religion is mere folly and the faith of the church a fable. True Christians must despise these grinning impostors. Exorcisms, then, were employed. The demon, forced to manifest himself, yielded his name. He began by giving these girls the most horrible convulsions; he went so far as to raise from the earth the body of the Superior who was being exorcised, and to reply to secret thoughts, which were manifested neither in words nor by any exterior signs. Questioned according to the form prescribed by the ritual, as to why he had entered the body of the nun, he replied, it was from hatred. But when, being questioned as to the name of the magician, he answered that it was Urbain Grandier, profound astonishment seized Canon Mignon and his assistants. They had indeed looked upon Grandier as a scandalous priest; but never had they imagined that he was guilty of Magic. They were therefore not satisfied with one single questioning: they repeated the interrogatory several times, and always received the same reply.

END OF VOL. I.

FOOTNOTES:

2.   Our author takes care not to mention that the Bishop of the Diocese was Grandier's greatest enemy.

3.   Huguenots, the name given to the early adherents of the Reformation in France. The origin of the word has been variously accounted for, but it was most probably introduced from Germany as a corruption of the German-Swiss *Eidgenossen*, confederates, or those bound together by an oath. Like many other names it was first given by opponents as a badge of reproach, and subsequently became honourable from its associations. The movement of the Reformation made its appearance in France at the beginning of the sixteenth century; and at the period when Luther was defending its principles before the Diet of Worms, Briconnet, bishop of Meaux, Lefevre, and Farel were labouring zealously for the same cause in France. At first the new doctrines, which seemed to be chiefly directed against the more open sins and derelictions of the clergy, enjoyed the toleration of the king, Francis I. and his sister Margaret of Valois, the queen of Navarre, was an active supporter of the cause. As it progressed however, the alarm and anger of the clergy became fully aroused, and as some of its manifestations had given offence to the king, a determined effort was made to extirpate it by means of fire and sword. In 1535 a solemn procession in vindication of the faith was made at Paris, in which the king walked bareheaded and bearing a taper; as part of the proceedings six Lutherans were burned, having their tongues cut out and being affixed to a movable gallows, which alternately rose and fell over a fire kindled beneath. This was followed by many executions of a similar kind, and by the more wholesale slaughters which exterminated the Vaudois of Provence; but in spite of these persecutions the number of those who adopted the principles of the Reformation continually increased. Under the influence of Calvin, who took very great interest in the work of the Reformation in France, the French Protestants about the middle of the sixteenth century began to organize themselves into churches, and to unite these churches into groups or districts for the purposes of mutual aid and counsel. The first French Protestant church was established at Paris in 1555, and very soon afterwards others were established in most of the large towns where the principles of the Reformation had obtained followers. These churches were established according to the Presbyterian form, a pastor being appointed as the leader, with elders and deacons to assist in the government and worship, each church being independent of the rest, though several churches might combine in any movement for their mutual benefit or for the promotion of their common cause. The first synod of the reformed churches was held at Paris in 1559. At this assembly, to which eleven churches sent deputies, a confession of faith and a series of articles of discipline were drawn up and issued, and these, with a few alterations, became subsequently the doctrinal and ecclesiastical standards of the Protestants of France. It is not easy to estimate the number of the Huguenots at this period, but according to Beza they were not less than 400,000, and the party included about one-third of the nobility of France. The persecutions of the Roman Catholic party, however, had become more fierce and intolerable as the number of the Protestants increased, and at last, driven to desperation, the Huguenots took up arms in their own defence and sought to change the government in order that they might gain liberty of worship. In February, 1560, at a meeting at Nantes, they resolved to petition the king, Francis II., for liberty of worship and for the removal of the two

brothers, Francis duke of Guise, and Charles of Lorraine, cardinal and archbishop of Rheims, who were the real rulers of the kingdom and the foremost in the persecution. In the event of a refusal they conspired to seize the person of the king and appoint their own leader, Louis I., prince of Bourbon Condé, as governor-general of the kingdom. The conspiracy failed completely, and a terrible vengeance was exacted: some 1200 of the Huguenots were slaughtered without investigation or trial, their bodies being flung into the Loire until the stream was almost choked by the number. In January, 1562, owing to political changes in France, Catherine de Médicis being obliged to rely upon the aid of the Protestant party in defence of her son Charles IX., who was under age, an edict was issued which gave the Huguenot noblemen the right to the free exercise of their religion on their own estates. A few months only after this a party of Huguenot worshippers in the little town of Vassy, in the province of Champagne, were attacked by the Duke of Guise and his followers, sixty being slain upon the spot, and 200 more severely, some mortally, wounded. For this butchery he was received with acclamation by the people of Paris, and emboldened by his reception he seized upon the persons of the young king and the queen-mother, and proclaimed the Protestants rebels against the royal authority. The latter rallied round the standard raised by Condé at Orleans, and the civil war was commenced which was to devastate France for nearly thirty years. At the outset the Huguenots were defeated at Rouen, 11th September, 1562, and again at Dreux, 19th December, the same year. In 1563 the treaty of Amboise was concluded, but its stipulations were observed by neither party, and the war was soon recommenced, the Huguenots being again defeated 10th November, 1567, at St. Denis. Reinforced by aid from Germany, they were able to threaten Paris, but their leader Condé allowed himself to be again duped by Catherine de Médicis, and signed the peace of Longjumeau, "leaving his party at the mercy of their enemies, with no other security than the word of an Italian woman." The queen-mother, as soon as the pressure of danger was removed, promptly recommenced the persecution, and within a few months several thousands of the Huguenots were either assassinated or publicly executed. Condé and Coligny fled to La Rochelle, where they were joined by the Queen of Navarre and her son Henry, afterwards Henry IV. of France, at the head of 4000 men. Assistance was also received from Germany and England, and the third war of religion was begun. The Huguenots were defeated 13th March, 1569, at Jarnac, and again at Moncontour, 3rd October, 1569, but they managed to take Nîmes, relieve La Rochelle, and gain the victory of Luçon. Their successes led again to the proposal of terms of peace; and a treaty, in which an amnesty and the free exercise of their religion everywhere except at Paris was granted to the Protestants, was signed at St. Germain-en-Laye, 8th August, 1570.

As with the treaties previously signed, the queen-mother and the leaders of the Roman Catholic party had no intention of observing its conditions, but on the contrary they sought to obtain by treachery that which they had failed to procure by force of arms. In two years their plans were ripe for execution, and the leaders of the Huguenot party having been enticed to Paris, a general massacre of the Protestants was commenced on St. Bartholomew's Day, 24th August, 1572. In the ghastly slaughter that followed, according to the lowest computation, 30,000 of the Protestants of France were destroyed, but many historians place the number killed at a much higher figure. Most of the leaders of the Huguenot party were destroyed in the massacre, but the remainder rallied their scattered forces, and a fresh war was commenced which continued with but few intermissions until the accession of Henry of Navarre in 1589. His reign marks a tranquil period in the history of the French Protestants, and in 1598 they obtained the celebrated Edict of Nantes, which though it granted them less than they had anticipated, was yet for a long period the foundation of their liberty. The period succeeding the reign of Henry IV. was marked by numerous outbreaks on the part of the Huguenots, who were distrustful of the plans and purposes of the French court, and ultimately Cardinal Richelieu determined to finally break their power by the capture of their chief stronghold, La Rochelle. This he effected in 1628, and with its fall and the subsequent surrender of the remaining Protestant towns the religious wars of France came finally to an end. Still the Huguenots were left in the enjoyment of freedom of religion, and being excluded from the court and service of the state, they devoted themselves to manufacture and commerce until they became the industrial leaders of the nation. They followed agriculture in the rural districts, and their farms were among the finest in France. The wine trade of Guienne, the cloths of Caen, the maritime trade on the sea-board of Normandy, the manufactures in the north-western provinces, the silk trade of Lyons, with many other branches of commerce, were almost entirely carried on by the Huguenots, who bore a high reputation for industry and integrity even among their enemies. The consolidation of the power of the king was, however, fraught with danger to the liberties of the Protestants, and as Louis XIV. in his declining years became morbidly superstitious, he sought, under the direction of Madame de Maintenon and his confessor Lachaise, to atone for his own crimes by the suppression of heresy. At first bribery was tried, and a regular fund of secret-service money was set apart for procuring conversions. Then persecution was recommenced, and many thousands were terrified into abjuring their religion by the means of the Dragonnades. Finally, in 1685 Louis revoked the Edict of Nantes, and followed up the revocation with laws of terrific severity against Protestantism. All Protestant worship was forbidden under penalty of arrest and confiscation of property. Ministers were to leave the kingdom within fourteen days unless they became converted. All Protestant schools were closed, and all children born after the passing of the law were to be baptized and brought up as Roman Catholics; all marriages, unless celebrated by the Roman Catholic clergy, were declared null, and the Protestant laity were strictly prohibited from leaving the kingdom.

The provisions of the edict were carried out with relentless rigour, and a desperate flight of the Huguenots ensued. Many thousands had been forced to emigrate by the dragonnades, but now the flight became wholesale, though every effort to check it was made by the authorities. Vauban, who wrote a year after the revocation, estimated the loss of France at 100,000 inhabitants, 60,000,000 francs in specie, 9,000 sailors, 12,000 veterans, 600 officers, and her most flourishing branches of manufacture and trade. Sismondi considers the loss to have exceeded 300,000 men, while some modern estimates put the number lost during the whole period of the persecution at not less than 1,000,000. A large number abjured their religion, but a remnant remained who neither fled nor abjured, and whose endurance and determination during the long years of persecution that followed form one of the most remarkable of the records of religious history. The loss of France was the enrichment of other lands, and England, America, Germany, Switzerland, Denmark, Sweden, and Holland all profited by the advent of the emigrants. It is estimated that during the ten years that followed the revocation nearly 80,000 of the Huguenots established themselves in England, and their influence upon the trade and manufactures of the country was both widespread and lasting. The long windows of the silk-weavers' houses still mark the quarter of Spitalfields, London, where not so very long since a considerable French colony, with English assistants, drove a thriving trade, though not a weaver is now to be found there.

The majority of the Huguenots, however, became merged in the general population of England, and their descendants heartily accepted the change of nationality. Many of the latter have since attained to eminence in their adopted country, and are to be found among the leaders of the nation in all branches of its activity. Similar results may be traced in other nations where the refugees took up their abode, and it is said that when the Emperor of Germany rode into Paris at the head of his victorious troops at the close of the war in 1871, not less than eighty members of his personal staff were descendants of the Huguenots who had been driven by persecution from France.

During the early part of the eighteenth century the rigour of the persecution was maintained, but gradually the spirit of the age began to be averse to such methods of maintaining the power of the priesthood, and the interference of Voltaire, after the judicial murder of John Calas, did much towards bringing the persecution to an end. In 1787 an edict of Louis XVI. restored civil rights to the Huguenots, and the Revolution of 1789 and the passing later of the Code Napoleon gave them equal rights with Roman Catholics. At the present time the Protestants of France number about 500,000, and many of their pastors receive a small salary from the state. They nevertheless enjoy a considerable amount of self-government, and they have an excellent reputation as industrious and orderly citizens. In the Protestant churches of France, as in those of other countries, there is a tendency to divide over the questions arising from the progress of scriptural and historical criticism. Some of the leaders are well known for the liberalism of their ideas, and for the work they have done in connection with the advancement of the science of theology, while others, fearing the Rationalizing tendencies of modern studies, cling more closely to the Calvinistic standards of their forefathers. [See "History of the Rise of the Huguenots," by Prof. M. Baird, 1880.]

4.   The friendship of the Bishop would account for Mignon's envy towards Grandier.

5.   When and under what circumstances confession, either public or private, was first deemed absolutely necessary for the remission of sins is a subject of controversy. Innocent III., in the fourth Lateran Council, A.D. 1215 (Canon 21), made confession (meaning auricular or private) obligatory upon every adult person once a year; and that continues to be one of the rules of the Roman Catholic church to the present day. The Council of Trent, in its Catechism, defines it to be "a declaration by the penitent of his sins made to a priest in order to receive the penance and absolution." Penitence, therefore, consists of four parts—confession, contrition, penance, and absolution; and it is a positive doctrine of the same church, that without the concurrence of all these parts or conditions the sacrament is null and void. The penance which the priest imposes consists generally of satisfaction to be given if the penitent has injured any one in his property, honour, &c., in a manner that can admit of reparation, and also of prayers, abstinence, or other religious practices to be performed. The secrecy imposed on confessors is strict and unconditional; whatever be the crime of

which a penitent may accuse himself, they are solemnly bound to keep it secret, under the most severe denunciations and penalties, both here and hereafter, that of excommunication included. The box in which the priest sits in the church to hear the penitent is called a confessional. But the act of confession may be performed out of church, in private houses, or in any place, in short, of which the bishop approves, provided it be not within hearing of any person except the priest and the penitent. The Greek Church retains the practice of auricular confession, but differs from that of Rome in the form of the absolution. The reformed churches do not as a rule encourage the practice, and in Scotland it is not even recognized. In the Church of England, although admitted by the Prayer Book, private confession has long been viewed with extreme suspicion, but of late years attempts have been made by a certain section to revive it.

6.   The reference is evidently to Mark XVI., p. 17 and 18.

PART II

THE DECLARATION OF the Evil Spirit could not fail to make a great commotion, and to have results which required precautions to be taken at once. The Canon, like a wise man, put himself in communication with Justice, and informed the magistrates of what was passing at the convent, on the 11th October, 1632. Grandier, prepared for all contingencies, had already taken his measures. Many of the magistrates belonged to the new religion and were favourable to him, looking upon him as a secret adherent; they served him as he expected. At the same time, he made all possible use of his extraordinary talents for pettifogging, presented petition on petition, questioned every statement of the exorcists and of the nuns, threatened their confessor Mignon, complained that his reputation was attacked, and that the means were thus taken from him of doing the good his position required, and demanded that the nuns should be locked up and the exorcisms be put an end to. He knew well enough that his demands were out of the question, and that civil justice has nothing to do with the exercise of religious functions. But he wished, if possible, to embarrass the exorcists, and commit the judges with the bishops, or, at any rate, throw discord among them, and give his Calvinists an opportunity of crying out; he succeeded.

The magistrates separated. Only those who were favourable to him remained: the rest ceased to appear at the exorcisms, and Mignon soon withdrew from the convent. Excitement rose in the public mind, a thousand arguments on this or that side permeated the town, and a thousand quarrels took place on all sides.

This excitement, however, and these disputes settled nothing, and the exorcisms, which continued, had no better result. Grandier triumphed, and his friends admired his wit, his skill, and proclaimed aloud that he could be convicted of nothing, not even as regards women, although they knew well how far he had gone in this matter. Until now, the Court had taken no notice of the affair; but the noise it had made in the world since the first days of October 1632 had reached the Queen's ears. She requested information, and the Abbé Marescot, one of her chaplains, was sent to examine into the matter and report to her. He arrived at Loudun on the 28th November, and witnessed what was going on. No immediate consequences followed: but an incident soon occurred, which caused a sudden change in the position of affairs.

The King had resolved to raze the castles and fortresses existing in the heart of the kingdom, and commissioned M. de Laubardemont to see to the demolition of that of Loudun. He arrived, and saw what a ferment the town was in, the animosity that reigned there, and the kind of man who caused the commotion. The complaints of those who were victims of the debaucheries, of the pride, or of the vengeance of the curate, touched him, and it seemed to him important to put an end to the scandal. On his return he informed the King and the Cardinal-Minister of the facts: Louis XIII., naturally pious and just, perceived the greatness of the evil, and deemed it his duty to put a stop to it. He appointed M. de Laubardemont to investigate the matter without appeal; with orders to choose in the neighbouring jurisdictions the most straightforward and learned judges. The Commission is dated 30th November, 1633.

Nothing less was needed to bring to justice a man upheld by a seditious and enterprising party, and so well versed in the details of *chicannerie*: an art always shameful in any man, but especially to an ecclesiastic. The King issued at the same time two decrees, to arrest and imprison Grandier and his accomplices. Armed with such powers, the Commissioner did not fear to attack a man who had so often succeeded in gaining either a nonsuit on some question of form, or in turning accusations to his own advantage, or else dragging out proceedings to such a length as to weary his adversaries and his judges.

The Calvinists, already irritated at the razing of the Castle which served them as a rallying place in times of rebellion, cried out against this new tribunal, because they saw that it was the sole means of rendering useless the knaveries of their friend. But they cried out much louder when the Commissioner arrested the accused, without waiting for informations, and seized all his papers. As if it were not well known that, in criminal matters, this mode of proceeding is usual. In this case it was absolutely necessary. For, without this precaution, Grandier might have fled, and defended himself from afar, engaging the attention of judges, who had plenty of work elsewhere. He might even have raised tumults in the city, which might have necessitated violent remedies.

These precautions being taken, the Commissioner commenced his investigation, and proceeded to hear witnesses on the 17th December, 1633.

The Commissioner now learned of what Grandier and his party were capable. The witnesses were so intimidated that none would speak, and it required all the Royal Authority to reassure them. He therefore issued a proclamation forbidding the intimidation of witnesses, under penalty of prosecution; and the Bishop of Poitiers having supported the King's decision, the two priests, Gervais Méchin and Martin Boulieau, who had been forced to retract their evidence in the former trial, presented a petition in which they declared that they had been seduced and constrained by several persons in authority to recall their evidence, and they now affirmed their first evidence to be true. The evidence of the nuns was also heard, and that of lay persons of both sexes, amongst others of two women, the one of whom confessed having had criminal relations with Grandier, and that he had offered to make her Princess of Magicians, whilst the second confirmed the evidence of the first.[7]

As regards the nuns, they deposed that Grandier had introduced himself into the convent by day and night for four months, without anyone knowing how he got in; that he presented himself to them whilst standing at divine service and tempted them to indecent actions both by word and deed; that they were often struck by invisible persons; and that the marks of the blows were so visible that the doctors and surgeons had easily found them, and that the beginning of all these troubles was signalized by the apparition of

Prior Moussaut, their first confessor. The Mother Superior and seven or eight other nuns, when confronted with Grandier, identified him, although it was ascertained that they had never seen him save by magic, and that he had never had anything to do with their affairs. The two women formerly mentioned and the two priests maintained the truth of their evidence. In a word, besides the nuns and six lay women, "sixty witnesses deposed to adulteries, incests, sacrileges, and other crimes, committed by the accused, even in the most secret places of his church, as in the vestry, where the Holy Host was kept, on all days and at all hours."

It may well be imagined that the mother, brothers and friends of the accused did not abandon him. They appealed to every possible authority. The details of these proceedings would be as wearisome as useless, as the Commissioner, by the very terms of his Commission, was placed above all such dilatory pettifogging, and therefore refused or annulled all applications in that direction. He then questioned the accused as to the facts and articles of accusation, and after having made him sign his confessions and denials, proceeded to Paris to inform the Court of what he had done.

The King and his Council thought it right to furnish him with means to overcome all obstacles to a speedy decision. This precaution was necessary, for letters from the Bailly of Loudun, Grandier's chief supporter, to the Procurator-General of the Parliament, were intercepted, in which it was asserted that the "possession" was an imposture. The latter's reply was also seized. Monsieur de Laubardemont returned therefore to Loudun with a Decree of the Council, dated 31st May 1634, confirming all his powers and *prohibiting Par-*

liament and all other judges from interfering in this business, and forbidding all parties concerned from appealing, under penalty of a fine of five hundred livres. He caused Grandier to be transferred from the prison of Augers to that of Loudun, so as to have him at hand to confront with witnesses, if need be.

But, first of all, he considered it necessary to examine the nuns carefully; for this purpose, with the consent of the Bishop, he sequestrated them in different convents, and interrogated them so severely that one might have thought that they themselves were the magicians. "He saw them all, the one after the other, for several days; and listened to their conversations, to observe their mode of thought. He enquired minutely into their lives, their morals, their behaviour, not only secular but religious. His depositions, or notes, which represented the evidence of twenty girls, including a few not nuns, filled fifty rolls of official paper, and were the admiration of all judges, so great was the prudence and care they demonstrated."

On the other hand the Bishop of Poitiers, after having sent several Doctors of Theology to examine the victims, came to Loudun in person, and exorcised them himself, or had them exorcised by others in his presence for two months and a half. Never was work done with such care and attention.

All precognitions over, the Commissioner began to confront the accused with the witnesses, and the latter maintained, face to face with Grandier, the evidence they had given against him.

As regard the nuns, it was observed that they never contradicted themselves, whether questioned together or separately, though they were examined often, by different persons, and as skilfully as possible. Now, criminals do not manage this, for the cleverest have the greatest difficulty in avoiding contradictory statements. Those writers, who have supported Grandier, have never discovered the least discrepancy in the evidence of the nuns. Nor did Grandier ever plead malice on their part as a defence, for they had never seen him, nor had he had anything to do with their affairs, as we have said.

If, as calumny asserts, the only thing sought was the death of Grandier, here were sufficient proofs to burn him, if only for abusing the privileges of his ministry and of his Church, or for the sacrileges he had committed therein. But justice is not satisfied with punishing one kind of crime, when she finds traces of another still more serious. It was moreover a Christian duty to assist the views of God, who permitted so strange an event, to confound the calumnies of the protestants, and to prove the demonstration the "possession" of the nuns, and the magic exercised by the accused. To this the Commissioners and the other judges applied themselves.

Thus, as it was a matter rather of religion than of jurisprudence, they resolved to begin by prayer to God, who is the Father of all Light, rightly considering that all France was watching the trial with eager eyes, that it was shrouded in a thick veil of obscurity, and that their verdict would entail important consequences. They therefore prepared to receive divine assistance and grace by frequent confessions, and by often receiving the Holy Sacrament. Then they decreed a general procession to implore celestial aid in so difficult a matter; and, to excite the devotion of the masses by their example, they went in a body, during the whole of the trial, to visit the Churches of the city, set aside by the Bishop for forty hour services, and reached each in time for the elevation of the host. Thence the Exorcists went to the Church fixed upon for the Exorcisms, and the judges proceeded to the tribunal to continue the case; in the evening all returned to church for evensong.

The examination lasted forty days, during which Demons gave them the clearest proofs of their presence in the bodies of the persons exorcised, and every day added new evidence against Grandier, and yet never said anything against him which did not turn out strictly true. These assertions merit distinct proof, which will be found interesting.

As regards the presence of Devils in the possessed, the Church teaches us in its ritual, that there are four principal signs, by which it can be undoubtedly recognised. These signs are the speaking or understanding of a language unknown to the person possessed; the revelation of the future, or of events happening far away; the exhibition of strength beyond the years and nature of the actor; and floating in the air for a few moments.

The Church does not require, in order to have recourse to Exorcisms, that all these marks should be found in the same subject; one alone, if well authenticated, is sufficient to demand public exorcism.

Now, they are all to be found in the Nuns of Loudun, and in such numbers that we can only mention the principal cases.

Acquaintance with unknown tongues first showed itself in the Mother-Superior. At the beginning, she answered in Latin the questions of the Ritual proposed to her in that language. Later, she and the others answered in any language they thought proper to question in.

M. de Launay de Razilli, who had lived in America, attested that, during a visit to Loudun, he had spoken to them in the language of a certain savage tribe of that country, and that they had answered quite correctly, and had revealed to him events that had taken place there.

Some gentlemen of Normandy certified in writing that they had questioned Sister Clara de Sazilli in Turkish, Spanish, and Italian, and that her answers were correct.

M. de Nismes, Doctor of the Sorbonne, and one of the chaplains of the Cardinal de Lyon, having questioned them in Greek and German, was satisfied with their replies in both languages.

Father Vignier, Superior of the Oratory at La Rochelle, bears witness in his Latin Narrative, that, having questioned Sister Elizabeth a whole afternoon in Greek, she always replied correctly and obeyed him in every particular.

The Bishop of Nimes commanded Sister Clara in Greek to raise veil and to kiss the railings at a certain spot; she obeyed, and did many other things he ordered, which caused the prelate to exclaim that one must be an Atheist or lunatic not to believe in "possession."

Some doctors questioned them also as to the meaning of some Greek technical terms, extremely difficult to explain, and only known to the most learned men, and they clearly expressed the real signification of the words.

Lastly, Grandier himself being confronted with them, his Bishop invested him with the stole to exorcise the Mother Superior, who, he declared, knew Latin; but he did not dare to question her or the others in Greek, though they dared him to it; whereon he remained very embarrassed.[8]

As to the Revelation of hidden matters or of events passing afar off, proofs are still more abundant. We will only select a few of the most remarkable.

M. Morin, Prior of St. Jacques de Thouars, having requested M. Morans, Commissioner appointed by the Bishop of Poitiers to watch over the possessed, and to assist in the trial of Grandier, to allow some sign to be given proving *actual infernal possession*, whispered to M. de Morans that he wished one of the possessed to bring him five rose leaves. Sister Clara was then away in the refectory; M. de Morans ordered, in his thoughts, the Demon who possessed her to obey the wish of M. Morin, for the greater glory of God. Thereupon the Nun left the refectory, and went into the garden, whence she brought first a pansy and other plants, and presented them with roars of laughter, saying to M. de Morans: "Is that what you wish, father? I am not a Devil, to guess your thoughts."—To which he replied simply: "*Obedias*," obey. She then returned to the garden, and after several repetitions of the order, presented through the railings a little rose branch, on which were six leaves. The Exorcist said to her: "*Obedias punctualiter sub pœnâ maledictionis*," obey to the letter under penalty of malediction; she then plucked off one leaf, and offered the branch saying: "I see you will only have five; the other was one too many." The Prior was so convinced by what he saw, that he went out with tears in his eyes. An official report of the fact was drawn up.

Madame de Laubardemontalse tried the same experiment, in order to convince many sceptics who were present; and she was equally successful.

The *Lieutenant-Criminel* of Orleans, the President Tours, Lieutenant-General de S. Maixant, and myself [9] also had our curiosity gratified. I desired that Sister Clara should bring me her beads, and say an *Ave-Maria*. She first brought a pin, and then some aniseed; being urged to obey, she said: "I see you want something else," and then she brought me her beads and offered to say an *Ave-Maria*.

M. Chiron, Prior of Maillezais, desiring to strengthen his belief in demoniacal possession, begged M. de Morans to allow him to whisper to a third party the sign he required; and he thereon whispered to M. de Fernaison, Canon and Provost of the same Church, that he wished the nun to fetch a missal then lying near the door, and to put her finger on the introit of the mass of the Holy Virgin, beginning "Salve, Sancta parens." M. de Morans, who had heard nothing, ordered Sister Clara, who was likewise ignorant of what had been said, to obey the intentions of M. Chiron. This young girl then fell into strange convulsions, blaspheming, rolling on the ground, exposing her person in the most indecent manner, without a blush, and with foul and lascivious expressions and actions, [10] till she caused all who looked on to hide their eyes with shame. Though she had never seen the prior, she called him by his name, and said he should be her lover. It was only after many repeated commands, and an hour's struggling, that she took up the missal, saying: "I will pray." Then, turning her eyes in another direction, she placed her finger on the capital S at the beginning of the introit aforesaid, of which facts reports were drawn up.

M. de Milliere, a gentleman of Maine, certified that, being present at the Exorcism of Sister Clara, and on his knees, the Devil asked him whether he was saying a *De Profundis* for his wife, which was the case. The Marquis de la Mothe, son of M. de Parabel, governor of Poitou, certified that sister Louise de Nogeret had disclosed his most secret faults in the presence of Father Tranquille, and of Madame de Neuillant, his aunt.

The same M. de la Mothe also asked an Exorcist to make Sister Clara, who was in the convent, come out, kneel down, and say an Ave Maria; she came after repeated commands, and obeyed.

Chevalier de Meré, who was present, asked the Devil on what day he had last confessed. The Devil answered Friday. The Chevalier acknowledged this to be correct; whereupon Sister Clara withdrew. But as he wished to try the Devil again, he begged the exorcist to make her return, and whispered some words to the Marquis and the Monk, for the nun to repeat. The exorcist refused, as the words were indecent. He changed them, therefore, into *Pater, et Filius et Spiritus Sanctus!* He whispered these words so low, that the exorcist could hardly hear them. The nun, who was in another room, came at the command of the Father, and addressing the Chevalier, first said the indecent words the monk had refused, and then repeated several times *Gloria patri et filio et Spiritui Sancto*. She was ordered to say the words exactly as she had been desired, but she said she would not.

The Bishop of Nîmes, being present at an exorcism by Father Surin, begged him to order something in difficult Latin; and the Demon thereupon performed what was wanted.

A Jesuit wishing to try what so many people stated they had experienced, gave an inward order to a demon who had been exorcised; and then immediately another. In the space of a second he gave five or six orders, which he countermanded one after another; and thus tormented the Devil, who was ordered to obey his intentions. The Demon repeated his commands aloud, beginning by the first, and adding, "But you wont," and when he had come to the last he said, "Now let's see whether we can do this."

"When it rained," says Father Surin, "the Devil used to place the Mother Superior under the water spout. As I knew this to be a habit of his, I commanded him mentally to bring her to me; whereupon she used to come and ask me: 'What do you want.'"

Another thing which struck the Exorcists, was the instantaneous answers they gave to the most difficult questions of Theology, as to grace, the vision of God, Angels, the Incarnation and similar subjects, always in the very terms used in the schools.

The corporal effect of possession is a proof which strikes the coarsest minds. It has this other advantage, that an example convinces a whole assembly.[11]

Now the nuns of Loudun gave these proofs daily. When the Exorcist gave some order to the Devil, the nuns suddenly passed from a state of quiet into the most terrible convulsions, and without the slightest increase of pulsation. They struck their chests and backs with their heads, as if they had had their neck broken, and with inconceivable rapidity; they twisted their arms at the joints of the shoulder, the elbow and the wrist two or three times round; lying on their stomachs they joined their palms of their hands to the soles of their feet; their faces became so frightful one could not bear to look at them; their eyes remained open without winking; their tongues issued suddenly from their mouths, horribly swollen, black, hard, and covered with pimples, and yet while in this state they spoke distinctly; they threw themselves back till their heads touched their feet, and walked in this position with wonderful rapidity, and for a long time. They uttered cries so horrible and so loud that nothing like it was ever heard before; they made use of expressions so indecent as to shame the most debauched of men, while their acts, both in exposing themselves and inviting lewd behaviour from those present, would have astonished the inmates of the lowest brothel in the country; they uttered maledictions against the three Divine Persons of the Trinity, oaths and blasphemous expressions so execrable, so unheard of, that they could not have suggested themselves to the human mind. They used to watch without rest, and fast five or six days at a time, or be tortured twice a day as we have described during several hours, without their health suffering; on the contrary, those that were somewhat delicate, appeared healthier than before their possession.

The Devil sometimes made them fall suddenly asleep: they fell to the ground and became so heavy, that the strongest man had great trouble in even moving their heads. Françoise Filestreau having her mouth closed, one could hear within her body different voices speaking at the same time, quarrelling, and discussing who should make her speak.

Lastly, one often saw Elizabeth Blanchard, in her convulsions, with her feet in the air and her head on the ground, leaning against a chair or a window sill without other support.

The Mother Superior from the beginning was carried off her feet and remained suspended in the air at the height of 24 inches. A report of this was drawn up and sent to the Sorbonne, signed by a great number of witnesses, ecclesiastics and doctors, and the judgement thereon of the Bishop of Poitiers who was also a witness. The doctors of the Sorbonne were of the same opinion as the Bishop, and declared that infernal possession was proved.

Both she and other nuns lying flat, without moving foot, hand, or body, were suddenly lifted to their feet like statues.

In another exorcism the Mother Superior was suspended in the air, only touching the ground with her elbow.

Others, when comatose, became supple like a thin piece of lead, so that their body could be bent in every direction, forward, backward, or sideways, till their head touched the ground; and they remained thus so long as their position was not altered by others.

At other times they passed the left foot over their shoulder to the cheek. They passed also their feet over their head till the big toe touched the tip of the nose.

Others again were able to stretch their legs so far to the right and left that they sat on the ground without any space being visible between their bodies and the floor, their bodies erect and their hands joined.

One, the Mother Superior, stretched her legs to such an extraordinary extent, that from toe to toe the distance was 7 feet, though she was herself but 4 feet high.

But sometime before the death of Grandier, this lady had a still stranger experience. In a few words this is what happened: In an exorcism the Devil promised Father Lactance as a sign of his exit, that he would make three wounds on the left side of the Mother Superior.

He described their appearance and stated the day and hour when they would appear. He said he would come out from within, without affecting the nun's health, and forbade that any remedy should be applied, as the wounds would leave no mark.

On the day named, the exorcism took place; and as many doctors had come from the neighbouring towns to be present at this event, M. de Laubardemont made them draw near, and permitted them to examine the clothes of the nun, to uncover her side in the presence of the assembly, to look into all the folds of her dress, of her stays which were of whalebone, and of her chemise, to make sure there was no weapon: she only had about her her scissors, which were given over to another. M. de Laubardemont asked the doctors to tie her; but they begged him to let them first see the convulsions they had heard spoken of. He granted this, and during the convulsions the Superior suddenly came to herself with a sigh, pressed her right hand to her left side and withdrew it covered with blood. She was again examined, and the doctors with the whole assembly saw three bloody wounds, of the size stated by the Devil; the chemise, the stays, and the dress were pierced in three places, the largest hole looking as if a pistol bullet had passed through. The nun was thereupon entirely stripped, but no instrument of any description was found upon her. A report was immediately drawn up, and *Monsieur*, brother of the King, who witnessed the facts, with all the nobles of his Court, attested the document.

END OF VOL. II.

7.   Our forefathers, if not more moral than ourselves, certainly punished immorality, *when discovered*, much more severely, as is witnessed by the following proclamation:—

"William by the Grace of God, King of Great Britain, France and Ireland, Defender of the Faith; To ... Macers of Our Privy Council, Messengers at Arms, Our Sherifs in that part, conjunctly and severally, specially constitute, Greeting: Forasmuch as, notwithstanding of the many good Laws and Acts of Parliament made against Prophaneness, and for the restraining and suppressing of Vice and Immoralities, the same do still abound, to the great dishonour of God, the Reproach of the true Protestant Religion, and to the hurt and prejudice of the Peace and Government of the Realm; And We being resolved, as it hath alwise been Our Care, to have these Laws and Acts of Parliament put in due and vigorous Execution; And conceiving that the Printing and publishing of an abreviat of the saids Acts duely collected, and laid together, for the better Information and Instruction of all Our Judges, Officers and Ministers of the Law, and also of all Our other good Subjects, may be of special Use and Advantage, for their better Observation and Execution, according, to their full Tenor and Intent: Therefore, and in Answer to an Address, presented to the Lords of Our Privy Council, by the Commissioners of the late General Assembly of this Church for that effect; We with Advice of the saids Lords of Our Privy Council, have thought fit, and do hereby appoint the Abreviat and List of the saids Acts hereto subjoined to be Printed and duely published at all the Mercat Crosses of the Head Burghs of the Shires, Stewartries, Regalities and Baillaries of this Realm: And farder, that in all time coming, this present Proclamation, with the Abreviat and List thereto subjoined, be publickly read twice every Year in all the Paroch Churches and Congregations within this Kingdom, to wit, on the first Lords Day after each Term of Whitsunday and Martinmas yearly, after the Forenoons Sermon, and before the dissolving of the Congregation; and that all Presbyteries be careful to have this Publication constantly and solemnly made in all Churches within their Bounds, with suitable and pertinent Exhortations, as they will be answerable; And We peremptorly Command and Charge, all Judges, Magistrats and Officers of the Law whatsoever, each of them within their Bounds and Jurisdictions; and as they are thereto respectively impowered, to be careful to put the foresaids Laws above, and after mentioned, to due and exact Execution upon their highest peril. Follows the List and Abbreviat of the Laws against Prophaneness, and for suppressing of Vice and Immorality. 1mo. Act twenty one, Charles second, Parliament first, Session first, Entituled, Act against the Crime of Blasphemy, that whosoever not being distracted in his Wits, shall rail upon, or Curse God, or any of the Persons of the Blessed Trinity, shall be processed before the Chief Justice, and being found Guilty, shall be punished with Death: As also, whosoever shall deny God, or any of the Persons of the Blessed Trinity; and obstinatly continue therein, being processed and found Guilty, shall be punished with Death. Item, The Act of Our first Parliament, Session fifth, Cap. Eleventh, Ratifying the foresaid Act; And farder Statuting, that whoever hereafter shall in their Writing or Discourse, Deny, Impugn or Quarel, Argue or Reason against the Being of God, or any of the Persons of the Blessed Trinity, or the Authority of the Holy Scriptures of the Old and New Testament, or the Providence of God, in the Government of the World, shall for the first Fault be punished with Imprisonment, ay and while they give publick Satisfaction in Sackcloth to the Congregation in which the

Scandal was committed; And for the second Fault, the Delinquent shall be fined in a years valued Rent of his real Estate, and the twenty part of his free personal Estate, the equal half of which Fines to be applyed to the Poor of the Paroch where the Crime shall be committed, and the other half to the Informer, besides his being Imprisoned, ay and while he again make Satisfaction as above; And for the third Fault, he shall be punished by Death, as an obstinat Blasphemer: And all Magistrats and Ministers of the Law, and Judges in this Kingdom, are Authorised and Required to put this Act in Execution as to the first Fault, as are all Sheriffs, Stewarts, Baillies of Baillaries and Regalities, and their Deputs, and Magistrats of Burghs, to put the same in Execution as to the second Fault; remitting the Execution thereof, as to the third Fault, to the Lords of His Majesties Justiciary. 2do. All Laws and Acts of Parliament made against Cursing and Swearing, as Act Queen Mary, Parliament fifth, Cap. Sixteenth, whereby it is Statute, that whosoever Swears abominable Oaths, and detestable Execrations, shall be punished with the Pecuniary Mulcts, and other pains contained in the said Act. Act James sixth, Parliament seventh, Cap. One hundred and third, ratifying the foresaid Act, with an Augmentation of the Pains, and that Censors be appointed in the Mercat place of all Burrows, and other publick Fairs, with Power to put the Swearers of abominable Oaths in Ward, while they have payed the saids Pains, and find Surety to abstain in time coming, and that by Direction and Commission of the Sherifs, Stewarts, Baillies, Provosts, Baillies of Burrows, Lords of Regalities, and other ordinary Officers; And that all House-holders delate to the Magistrates, the Names of the Transgressors of this present Act within their Houses, that they may be punished, under the pain to be esteemed and punished as Offenders themselves; And that if the said Magistrats be remiss or negligent in the Execution of this Act, they shall upon Complaint be called before Us, and Our Privy Council, and committed to Ward during pleasure, and find Surety under great Pains at Our sight, for their exact Diligence in executing the said Act thereafter. Act Charles second, Parliament first, Session first, Cap. nineteenth, ratifying and approving all Acts of Parliament against all manner of Cursing and Swearing. And farder declaring that each Person who shal Blaspheme, Swear or Curse, shall be lyable in the pains following, each Nobleman in twenty Pounds Scots, each Baron in twenty Merks, each Gentleman, Heretor or Burges in ten Merks, each Yeoman in forty shillings Scots, each Servant in twenty shillings *toties quoties*, each Minister in the fifth part of his Years Stipend, and if the Party Offender be not able to pay the Penalties foresaid, then to be examplary punished in his Body, according to the Merit of his Fault: And this Act is again Ratified, Charles second, Parliament second, Session third, Cap. twenty two, which contains a distinct and particular Method, how and by whom, it shall be Execute. 3tio. All Laws and Acts of Parliament for Observation of the Sabbath or Lords-Day, As Act James sixth, Parliament sixth, Cap. seventy one, That there be no Mercats nor Fairs holden upon the Sabbath Day, nor yet within the Kirk or Kirk-yards that Day, or any other day; and that no Handy-Labour be used upon the Sabbath-Day, under the pain of Ten shilling Scots; and that no Gaming, Playing, passing to the Taverns and Ale Houses, or selling of Meat or Drink, or wilful remaining from the Paroch-Kirk in time of Sermon, or Prayers, upon the Sabbath-Day be used, under the Pains of Twenty shilling Scots, and who refuse, or are unable to pay the saids Pains, shall be put and holden in the Stocks, or such other Engine devised for publick Punishment, by the space of Twenty Four Hours; and this Act as to the discharging of Fairs and Mercats holden on Sabbath-Days, Ratified James the Sixth, Parliament Thirteenth, Cap. one hundred and fifty nine, and again Ratified against these who Prophane the Sabbath-Day, by Selling or Presenting Goods to be sold upon the said Day, and the Pain of the Third Transgression, declared to be Escheat of their haill Goods and Punishment of their Persons at our Will; James sixth, Parliament fourteenth, Cap. one hundred and ninety eight. Item, Act eighteenth Charles second, Parliament first, Entituled, Act for the due Observation of the Sabbath-Day, Ratifying and Approving all former Acts of Parliament made for Observation of the Sabbath-Day, and against the Breakers thereof, and discharging all going of Salt pans, Milns or Kilns, under the pain of twenty Pounds Scots, to be payed by the Heretors and Possessors thereof; and all Salmond-fishing, hiring of Shearers, carrying of Loads, keeping of Mercats, or using of Merchandice on the said Day, and all other Prophanations thereof, under the pain of Ten Pounds Scots, the one half whereof to be payed by the said Fisher, and Shearer hired, and the other half by the persons Hiring, and if the Offender be not able to pay the saids Penalties, that he be exemplary punished in his Body, according to the Merit of his Fault; and this Act ratified Charles second, Parliament second, Session third, Cap. twenty two. 4to. The Act Charles second, Parliament first, Session first, Cap. twenty, Entituled, Act against Cursing and Beating of Parents, whereby it is Statute, that whosoever Son or Daughter above the age of sixteen years, not being distracted, shall Beat and Curse either their Father or Mother, shall be put to death without Mercy, and such as are within the Age of Sixteen Years, and past the Age of Pupilarity, to be punished at the Arbitrament of the Judge, according to their deserving. 5to. All Acts against Drunkards and excessive Drinking, such as the Act James sixth, Parliament twenty two, Cap. twenty whereby it is Statute, That all persons convict of Drunkenness, or of Haunting of Taverns and Ale-Houses after Ten Hours at Night, or at any time of the Day, except in time of Travel, or for ordinary Refreshment, shall for the first Fault pay Three Pounds, or if unable, or refusing, be put in Joggs or Prison for the space of six Hours; For the second Fault five Pounds, or if unable, or refusing, to be keeped in Stocks or Prison for the space of twelve Hours; And for the third Fault, to pay Ten Pounds, or in case foresaid to be keeped in Stocks or Prison for the space of twenty four Hours: if they transgress thereafter, to be committed to Prison till they find Caution for their good Behaviour. Item, The Act Charles second, Parliament first, Cap. nineteenth, Ratifying all former Acts against the Crime of excessive Drinking, Declaring, That whosoever shall drink unto Excess, shall be lyable, each Nobleman in twenty pounds Scots, each Baron in twenty Merks, each Gentleman, Heretor or Burgess in ten Merks, each Yeoman in forty shillings, each Servant in twenty shillings Scots *toties quoties*; each Minister in the fifth part of his years Stipend, and that the Offender unable to pay the foresaids Penalties be exemplary punished in his Body, according to the Merit of his Fault. 6to. The Laws and Acts of Parliament made against Adulterers, as Queen Mary, Parliament fifth, Cap. twenty, whereby it is Statute, That manifest and incorrigible Adulterers after the Process of Haly-Kirk, sua far as the samen may extend, is used upon them, for their Disobedience and Contemption, be denounced Rebels and put to the Horn, and all their Moveable inbrought as Escheat, and no Appellation interponed frae the said Censures of Haly-Kirk to suspend the Horning. Act Queen Mary, Parliament ninth, Cap. seventy four, That all notour and manifest Committers of

Adultery be punished with all rigour unto the Death, as well the Woman as the Man, after due Monition made to abstain frae the said nottour Crime, and that for other Adultery the Acts and Laws made thereupon of before, be put to Execution with all rigour. And the Act James sixth, Parliament seventh, Cap. one hundred and fifth, whereby it is declared, That it shall be judged nottour and manifest Adultery, wordie of the pain of Death, whoever has Bairns one or moe procreat betwixt the persons Adulterers, or when they keep Company in Bed together notoriously known, or when they are suspect of Adultery, and duely admonished by the Kirk, to abstain and satisfy the Kirk by Repentance and Purgation, yet contemptuously refusing, are Excommunicat for their Obstinacy. 7timo. All Laws and Acts of Parliament made against Fornication, as Act Ja. sixth, Parliament first, Cap. thirteenth, Statuting, That who shall commit the filthy Vice of Fornication, shall for the first Fault, as well the Man as the Woman, pay the Sum of Forty pounds, or then both he and she shall be Imprisoned for the space of eight days, their Food to be Bread and small Drink, and thereafter presented to the Mercat-place of the Town or Paroch bare-headed, shall there stand fastned, that they may not remove for the space of two Hours; For the second Fault, the Sum of one hundred Merks, or then the forenamed days of their Imprisment shall be doubled, their Food to be Bread and Water allenarly, and thereafter shall be presented to the Mercat-place, and the Heads of both the Man and the Woman to be Shaven. And for the third Fault, One hundred Pounds, or else the above Imprisonment to be Tripled, their Food to be Bread and Water allenarly; And thereafter to be taken to the deepest and foulest Pool or Water of the Town or Paroch, and there to be thrice Doucked, and then Banished the said Town and Paroch, for ever, and how oft any Person shall be Convict thereafter of the said Vice of Fornication, that so oft the third Penalty be Execute upon them. Item, The Act Charles second, Parliament first, Cap. Thirty Eight, Impowering the Justices of Peace to put in Execution Acts of Parliament, for punishing the persons Guilty of Fornication, and that they cause them pay the Pecunial Sums following: Each Nobleman for the first Fault, Four hundred Pounds; Each Baron Two hundred Pounds; Each other Gentleman or Burges, One hundred Pounds. Every other person of Inferior Quality Ten Pounds Scots Money, and that these Penalties be doubled *toties quoties*, according to the Relapses, and Degrees of the Offence, and Quality of the Offenders; And that they be payed not only by the Man, but also by the Woman according to her Quality, and the Degree of her Offence, the one without prejudice of the other. Item, the said Act Charles second, Parliament first, Session first, Cap. thirty eight, Statutes, That the Justices of Peace put in Execution all Acts of Parliament for punishing all persons, who shall be Mockers, or Reproachers of Piety, or the Exercise thereof, and cause them pay the Penalties contained in the forementioned Act of Parliament against prophane Swearing. Item, The Act of our first Parliament, Session fifth, Cap. Thirteenth, Entituled, Act against Prophaneness, strictly requiring and enjoining, that all Sherifs and their Deputs, Stewarts and their Deputs, Baillies of Baillaries, and their Deputs, Magistrats of Burghs-Royal, and Justices of Peace within whose Bounds any of the said Sins of Cursing, Swearing, Drunkenness, Fornication, Prophanation of the Lords Day, and Mocking and Reproaching of Religion shall happen to be committed, to put the saids Acts to exact and punctual Execution at all times, without necessity of any Dispensation, and against all persons, whether Officers, Soldiers or others without Exception; Certifying, that such of the saids Judges as shall refuse, neglect, or delay to put the Laws made against the said Sins in Execution, upon application of any Minister or Kirk-Session, or any person in their Name offering Information, and sufficient Probation, shall *toties quoties* be subject and liable to a Fine of an hundred pounds Scots, for which they may be pursued at the instance of the Agent of the Kirk, or Minister of the Paroch by summar Process, without the Order of the Roll. Item, the Twenty one Act of the second Session of the current Parliament, dated the nineteenth of July One thousand six hundred and ninety, Entituled, Act anent Murdering of Children, whereby it is Statute, That if any Woman shall conceal her being with Child during the whole space, and shall not call for, and make use of Help and Assistance in the Birth, the Child being found Dead or Amissing, the Mother shall be holden and repute the Murderer of her own Child, tho there be no appearance of Bruise or Wound upon the Body of the Child.[1] All which Acts abovementioned are hereby ordered to be published only for superabundance, and the better Information of our Liedges, without the least derogation to other Acts or Laws not published in this manner. Our Will is Herefore, and we Charge you strictly and Command, that incontinent these our Letters seen ye pass to the Mercat Cross of Edinburgh, and to the remanent Mercat Crosses of the Head Burghs of the several Shires, and Stewartries within this Kingdom, and in Our Name and Authority make Publication hereof, that none may pretend Ignorance; And We Ordain Our Solicitor, to dispatch Copies hereof, to the Sherifs of the several Shires, and Stewarts of Stewartries and their Deputs or Clerks to be by them published at the Mercat Crosses of the Head Burghs upon Receit thereof, and immediately sent to the several Ministers, to the effect the same may be read and intimate at their Paroch Churches, upon the Lords Day immediately following Footnote: the Publication hereof at the said Mercat Crosses. And Ordains these Presents to be Printed and Published in manner foresaid.

"Given under Our Signet at Edinburgh the twenty fifth day of January, and of Our Reign the ninth year, 1698.

"*Per Actum Dominorum Secreti Concilii.*

"Gilb. Eliot. *Cls. Sti. Concilii.*"

8.   How many of our learned clergy could to-day question anyone in Greek, and how would many of our bishops feel if they knew that their reputations and lives depended on their carrying on a conversation in the languages of Hellas?

9.   We learn from the "Démonomanie" that M. des Niau was the person here referred to in the first person, and therefore the writer of the book.

10.   The text says: "Relevant jupes et chemise, montrant ses parties les plus secretes, sans honte, et se servant de mots lascifs. Ses gestes devinrent si grossiers que les témoins se cachaient la figure. Elle répétait, en s' ... des mains, "Venez donc, f ... moi!"

11.   A curious case is mentioned in Arnot's Criminal Trials:—

"In 1697 an impostor appeared, in the character of a person tormented by witches, Christian Shaw, daughter of John Shaw of Bargarran, a gentleman of some note in the county of Renfrew. She is said to have been but eleven years of age. And although it is probable that hysterical affections may in part have occasioned her rhapsodies to proceed from real illusion, as well as accounted for the contortions which agitated her body; yet she seems to have displayed an artifice above her years, an address superior to her situation, and to have been aided by accomplices, which dulness of apprehension, or violence of prejudice, forbade the bystanders to discover.

"This actress was abundantly pert and lively; and her challenging one of the house-maids for drinking, perhaps for stealing, a little milk, which drew on her an angry retort, was the simple prelude to a complicated and wonderful scene of artifice and delusion, of fanaticism and barbarity.

"In the month of August 1696,[11] within a few days after her quarrel with the house-maid, the girl was seized with hysterical convulsions, which in repeated fits displayed that variety of symptoms which characterise this capricious disease. To these, other appearances were speedily added, which could only be attributed to supernatural influence, or to fraud and imposition. She put out of her mouth quantities of egg-shells, orange-pill, feathers of wild, and bones of tame fowl, hair of various colours, hot coal-cinders, straws, crooked pins, &c.

"Having by those sensible objects impressed the publick with the most complete and fearful conviction of her being 'grievously vexed[111] with a Devil,' she found herself capable to command the implicit assent of the spectators, in matters that were repugnant to the evidence of their own senses. For this purpose, she fell upon the device of seeming to possess the faculties of seeing and hearing, in a manner opposite to that of the rest of mankind. She would address some invisible beings as if actually present; at other times, in her conversations with those invisible beings, she would rail at them for telling her that persons actually present were in the room; protesting that she did not see them, yet at the same time minutely describing their dress. For instance, she spake as follows to the chief of her alledged tormentors, Catherine Campbell, with whom she had the quarrel, and who, to use the language of those times, was not *discernibly* present: 'Thou sittest with a stick in thy hand to put into my mouth, but thorough God's strength thou shalt not get leave: Thou art permitted to torment me, but I trust in God thou shalt never get my life. I'll let thee see, *Kattie*, there is no repentance in hell. O what ailed thee to be a witch! Thou sayest it is but three nights since thou wast a witch. O, if thou would'st repent, it may be God might give thee repentance, if thou would'st seek it, and *confess*; if thou would desire me, I would do what I could; for the Devil is an ill master to serve,' &c. &c. After that, she took up her Bible, read passages, and expounded them; and, upon one's offering to take it from her, she shrieked horribly, exclaiming, 'She would keep her Bible in spite of all the Devils in hell!' Then she fought, and kicked, and writhed herself, as if struggling with some invisible tormentor. When the sheriff-depute of the county, accompanied by a macer of Justiciary, came to apprehend some of the persons whom her diabolical malice had accused, and were actually in her presence, she addressed an imaginary and invisible correspondent thus: 'Is the sheriff come? Is he near me?' (Then stretching forth her hand, as if to grope, and the sheriff putting his hand into hers, she proceeded:) '*I cannot feel the sheriff.* How can he be present here? or how can I have him by the hand, as thou sayest, seeing I feel it not? Thou sayest he has brown coloured cloaths, red plush breeches, with black stripes, flowered muslin cravat, and an embroidered sword-belt: Thou sayest there is an old gray haired man with him, having a ring upon his hand; but I can neither see nor feel any of them. What, *are they come to apprehend the gentlewoman?* Is this their errand indeed?'

"These reiterated and aweful exercises of the dominion of Satan (for such they were universally deemed), impressed all ranks with amazement and terror. The clergy, as was their duty, were the foremost to embrace the cause of a disciple that was engaged *in more than spiritual* warfare with the grand enemy. Clergymen, by rotation, attended the afflicted damsel, to assist the minister of the parish, the family of Bargarran, and other pious Christians, in the expiatory offices of fasting and prayer. A publick fast was ordained by authority of the presbytery. Three popular clergymen successively harangued the trembling audience; and one of them chose for his theme this awful text, "Woe to the inhabitants of the earth and of the sea, for the Devil is come down unto you, having great wrath, because he knoweth that he hath but a short time. *And when the dragon saw that he was cast down unto the earth, he persecuted the woman.*"[IV] And the prayers and exhortations of the church were speedily seconded with the weight of the secular arm.

"On the 19th of January, a warrant of Privy Council was issued,[V] which set forth, that there were pregnant grounds of suspicion of witchcraft in the shire of Renfrew, especially from the afflicted and extraordinary condition of Christian Shaw, daughter of John Shaw of Bargarran. It therefore granted commission to Alexander Lord Blantyre, Sir John Maxwell of Pollock, Sir John Shaw of Greenock, William Cunnyngham of Craigens, Alexander Porterfield of Duchall, —— Caldwall of Glanderstoun, Gavin Cochrane of Thornlymuir, Alexander Porterfield of Fullwood, and Robert Semple sheriff-depute of Renfrew, or any five of them, to interrogate and imprison persons suspected of witchcraft, to examine witnesses, &c. but not upon oath, and to transmit their report before the 10th of March. The act of Privy Council is subscribed thus, 'Polwarth *Cancellar*, Argyle, Leven, Forfar, Raith, Belhaven, Ja. Steuart, J. Hope, W. Anstruther, J. Maxwell, Ro. Sinclair.'

"In the report which was presented on the 9th of March, the commissioners represented that there were 'twenty-four persons male and female suspected and accused of witchcraft,' and that further inquiry ought to be made into this crime. Among these unhappy objects of suspicion, it is to be remarked, that there was 'a girl of fourteen, and a boy not twelve years of age.' Agreeable to this report, a new warrant was issued by the Privy Council to most of the commissioners formerly named, with the addition of Lord Hallcraig, Mr. Francis Montgomery of Giffin, Sir John Houston of that Ilk, Mr John Kincaid of Corsbasket, Advocate, and Mr John Stewart younger of Blackhall, Advocate, or any five of them, to meet at Renfrew, Paisley, or Glasgow, to take trial of judge, and do justice upon the foresaid persons; and to sentence the guilty 'to be burned or otherwise executed to death,' as the commissioners should incline. It further ordained the commissioners to transmit to the Court of Justiciary an authentick extract of their proceedings, to be entered upon its records; and contained a recommendation to the Lords of the Treasury to defray the expences of the trial. The act is subscribed, 'Polwarth *Cancellar*, Douglass, Lauderdale, Annandale, Yester, Kintore, Carmichael, W. Anstruther, Arch. Mure.'

"The commissioners, thus empowered, were not remiss in acting under the authority delegated to them. After twenty hours were spent in the examination of witnesses, who *gave testimony* that the *malefices*[VI] libelled could not have proceeded from natural causes, and that the prisoners were the authors of these malefices.—After five of the unhappy prisoners confessed their own guilt, and criminated their alledged associates—after counsel had been heard on both sides, and the counsel for the prosecution had declared, that 'he would not press the jury with the *ordinary severity* of threatening an *assize of error*:[VII] But recommended to them to proceed according to the evidence; and loudly declared to them, that although they ought to beware of condemning the innocent, yet if they should acquit the prisoners, in opposition to legal evidence, 'they would be accessory to all the blasphemies, apostacies, murders, tortures, and seductions, whereof these enemies of heaven and earth should hereafter be guilty.' After the jury had spent six hours in deliberation, seven of those miserable persons were condemned to the flames.[VIII]

"The time however fast approached, when these human sacrifices were to be abolished. The last person who was prosecuted before the Lords of Justiciary for witchcraft was Elspeth Rule, who was tried before Lord Anstruther at the Dumfries circuit, on the 3d of May, 1709. [IX] No special act of witchcraft was charged against her; the indictment was of a very general nature, that the prisoner was 'habit and repute'[X] (that is, generally holden and deemed) a witch; and that she had used threatening expressions against persons at enmity with her, who were afterwards visited with the loss of cattle, or the death of friends, and one of whom run mad. The jury, by a majority of voices, found these articles proved, and the Judge ordained the prisoner to be burned on the cheek, and to be banished Scotland for life. The last person who was brought to the stake in Scotland for the crime of witchcraft was condemned by Captain David Ross of Little Daan[XI] sheriff-depute of Sutherland, A.D. 1722.

"Besides in the sufferings, and tragical end of the persons already specified, human ingenuity seems to have been exhausted in devising variety of torment, against other persons who lay under the suspicion of witchcraft, and who persisted, with astonishing fortitude, in denying the absurd imputation, even when urged with the sharpest tortures."

From the universal and excessive abhorrence entertained at a witch, a suspicion of that crime, independent of judicial severities,[XII] was sufficient to render the unhappy object anxious for death.—Thrusting of pins into the flesh, and keeping the accused from sleep, were the ordinary treatment of a witch. But if the prisoner was endued with uncommon fortitude, other methods were used to extort confession. The 'boots,' the 'caspie-claws,' and the 'pilniewinks,' engines for torturing the legs, the arms, and the fingers, were applied to either sex; and that with such violence, that sometimes the blood would have spouted from the limbs. Loading with heavy irons, and whipping with cords, till the skin and flesh were torn from the bones, have also been the adopted methods of torment.

The bloody zeal of those inquisitors attained to a refinement in cruelty so shocking to humanity,[XIII] and so repugnant to justice, as to be almost incredible. Not satisfied with torturing *the person* of the accused, their ingenious malice assailed the more delicate feelings, and ardent affections of the *mind*. An aged husband, an infant daughter, would have been tortured in presence of the accused, in order to subdue her resolution.—Nay, death itself[XIV] did not screen the remains of those miserable persons from the malice of their prosecutors. If an unfortunate woman, trembling at a citation for witchcraft, ended her sufferings by her own hands, she was dragged from her house at a horse's tail, and buried under the gallows.

I. This is the Act on which Sir Walter Scott founded his story of the "Heart of Mid-Lothian."
II. True narrative of the sufferings and relief of a young girl. Edinburgh, printed by James Watson, 1698.

III. St. Matthew, c. 15, v. 22.

IV. Revelations, chap. 12.

V. Records of Privy Council, January 19. March 9. April 5. 1697.

VI. "Malefice" in the Scots law signifies an act or effect of witchcraft.

VII. This was an oblique and most scandalous menace. "Assizes of Error" were declared a grievance by the Estates of Parliament at the Revolution.

VIII. The order of Privy Council for recording the Commissioners' proceedings in the books of Justiciary was not complied with. I am therefore unable to give any further particulars of the catastrophe of these miserable persons, or of the criminal absurdity of those who committed them to the flames.

IX. Records of Circuit Court of Justiciary, holden at Dumfries May 3, 1709.

X. "Habit and repute" is a very dangerous doctrine of the law of Scotland, at that time in full force, by which a man might be hanged altho' hardly any charge were exhibited against him, but that he had a bad character. For instance, if a man was charged with stealing a pair of old shoes, value threepence, and with being "habit and repute" a thief, if the jury found such indictment proved, or such prisoner guilty, the Court would by law be bound to sentence the prisoner to be hanged; if my temerity may be pardoned, for supposing that any such thing exists as a precise established rule of criminal law in Scotland.

XI. It is no small disappointment to me that I cannot lay this trial before the reader. The Sheriff Court books of the county of Sutherland were carried off by the Sheriff Clerk about 1735. I am somewhat however consoled for my disappointment, by the politeness shown me by James Traill, Esq. of Hobbister, Advocate, Sheriff-depute of Caithness and Sutherland, who was so obliging as to make a laborious but ineffectual search to recover the books.

XII. Mackenzie's Criminal Trials, tit. *Witchcraft*.

XIII. Records of Justiciary, June 24. 1596. When Alison Balfour was accused of witchcraft, she was put in the caspie-claws, where she was kept forty-eight hours; her husband was put in heavy irons, *her son put in the boots, where he suffered fifty-seven strokes*, and her little daughter, of about seven years of age, put in the pilniewinks, in her presence, in order to make her confess.—She did confess.—She retracted her confession in the course of the trial; and publickly, at her execution, declared that the confession was extorted from her by the torments.—The mode of tormenting and executing those miserable women is further illustrated by the authentic account of the expence of burning a witch at Burncastle, near Lauder, A.D. 1649.

XIV. Fountainhall's Decisions, vol. 1. p. 60. October 9. 1679.

PART III

ON FRIDAY THE 23rd of June, 1634, about three o'clock in the afternoon, the Bishop of Poitiers and M. de Laubardemont being present,
Grandier was brought from his prison to the Church of Ste. Croix
in his parish, to be present at the exorcisms. All the possessed were
there likewise. And as the accused and his partisans declared that
the possessions were mere impostures, he was ordered to be himself the exorcist, and the stole was presented to him. He could not
refuse, and therefore, taking the stole and the ritual, he received
the pastoral benediction, and after the *Veni Creator* had been sung,
commenced the exorcism in the usual form. But where he should
haughtily have given commands to the demon, instead of saying *Im-
pero*, I command, he said, *Cogor vos*, that is, I am constrained by you.
The Bishop sharply reprimanded him, and as he had said that some
of the possessed understood Latin, he was allowed to interrogate in
Greek. At the same time, the demon cried out by the mouth of Sister
Clara: "Eh! speak Greek, or any language you like; I will answer." At
these words, he became confused, and could not say anything more.

To behave thus, or to acknowledge the truth of the accusation, is one and the same thing, but other circumstances strengthened this certainty.

Any man whose own writing testifies against him is lost. Now this is what Grandier experienced. The devils, in several instances, confessed four pacts he had entered into.

This word, Pact, is somewhat equivocal. It may mean either the document by which a man gives himself to the devil, or the physical symbols, whose application will produce some particular effects in consequence of the pact. Here is an example of each case. Grandier's pact, or magical characters, whereby he gave himself to Beelzebub, was as follows:—"My Lord and Master, Lucifer, I recognise you as my God, and promise to serve you all my life. I renounce every other God, Jesus Christ, and all other Saints; the Catholic, Apostolic and Roman Church, its Sacraments, with all prayers that may be said for me; and I promise to do all the evil I can. I renounce the holy oil and the water of baptism, together with all the merits of Jesus Christ and his Saints; and should I fail to serve and adore you, and do homage to you thrice daily, I abandon to you my life as your due."

These characters were recognised as being in Grandier's own hand.

Now here is a specimen of the other kind of pact or magical charm. It was composed of the flesh of a child's heart, extracted in an assembly of magicians held at Orleans in 1631, of the ashes of a holy wafer that had been burnt, and of something else which the least straight-laced decency forbids me to name.

A most convincing proof of Grandier's guilt is that one of the devils declared he had marked him in two parts of his body. His eyes were bandaged and he was examined by eight doctors, who reported they had found two marks in each place; that they had inserted a needle to the depth of an inch without the criminal having felt it, and that no blood had been drawn. Now this is a most decisive test. For however deeply a needle be buried in such marks no pain is caused, and no blood can be extracted when they are magical signs.

But if the devils, overcome by the exorcisms, at times gave evidence against the criminal, at others they seemed to conspire to blacken him still more under the semblance of an apparent justification. Thus several of the possessed spoke in his favour: and some even went so far as to confess that they had calumniated him. Indeed, the Mother Superior herself, one day when M. de Laubardemont was in the convent, stripped herself to her shift, and, with a rope round her neck and a candle in her hand, stood for two hours in the middle of the yard, although it was raining heavily; and when the door of the room in which M. de Laubardemont was seated, was opened, she threw herself on her knees before him, declaring she repented of the crime she had committed in accusing Grandier, who was innocent. She then withdrew and fastened the rope to a tree in the garden, attempting to hang herself, but was prevented by the other nuns.

When the devil played these kind of tricks they forced him to retract, by calling on him to take Jesus Christ present in the Eucharist as witness of the truth of his statement, which he never dared to do.

What criminals could ever be condemned if such proofs were not deemed sufficient? The certainty of the possessions; the depositions of two priests who accused him of sacrilege; those of the nuns, declaring that they saw him day and night for four months, though the gates of the convent were kept locked; the two women who bore witness that he offered to make one of them Princess of the Magicians; the evidence of sixty other witnesses; his own embarrassment and confusion on so many occasions; the disappearance of his three brothers, who had fled and were never seen again; his pact and the magic characters that were afterwards burnt with him: all these placed his guilt beyond doubt.

The trial being completed, and the magician duly convicted, there only remained to sentence the evil doer. The Commissioners assembled at the Carmelite Convent, and it was noticed that there was not the slightest difference of opinion among all the fourteen judges, though they had never seen or known one another. They were all agreed as to the penalty to be inflicted, and having pronounced their sentence, they were filled with joy and their conscience was perfectly at rest. It was as if God, whose honour was so interested in this affair, had intended to give them this consolation.

No one among the Catholics, or, indeed, among all honest men, failed to applaud the sentence on Grandier. It was as follows:—

"We have declared, and declare the said Urbain Grandier attainted and convicted of the crimes of magic, maleficence and possession occurring through his act, in the persons of certain Ursuline Nuns of this town of Loudun, and other women; together with other crimes resulting therefrom. For reparation whereof we have condemned, and do condemn, the said Grandier to make 'amende honorable' bareheaded, a rope round his neck, holding in his hand a burning torch of the weight of two pounds, before the principal gate of Saint Pierre du Marché, and before that of Saint Ursula of the said town; and there, on his knees, to ask pardon of God, the King, and Justice, and that done, to be led to the public square of Sainte Croix, to be there tied to a stake, which for that purpose shall be erected in the said square, and his body to be there burnt with the pacts and magical inscriptions now in custody of the Court, together with the manuscript book written by him against the celibacy of priests, and his ashes to be scattered to the wind. We have declared all his property forfeited and confiscated to the Crown, less a sum of 150 livres, which shall be expended in the purchase of a copper plate, on which shall be engraved the present sentence, and the same shall be placed in a prominent position in the said Church of St. Ursula, there to be preserved for ever. And before this present sentence shall be carried out, we order that the said Grandier shall be put to the question ordinary and extraordinary, to discover his accomplices.—Pronounced at Loudun on the said Grandier, and executed the 18th of August, 1634."

In execution of this sentence, he was taken to the Court of Justice of Loudun. His sentence having been read to him, he earnestly begged M. de Laubardemont and the other Commissioners to mitigate the rigour of their sentence. M. de Laubardemont replied that the only means of inducing the judges to moderate the penalties was to declare at once his accomplices, and by some act of repentance for his past crimes to implore Divine mercy. The only answer he gave was, that he had no accomplices, which was false; for there is no magician but must be accompanied by others.

For the last forty days the Commissioner had placed at his side two monks to convert him. But all was in vain. Nothing could touch this hardened sinner. It is true, however, that the conversion of a magician is so rare an occurrence that it must be placed in the rank of miracles. "I am not astonished," says one who was present, "at his impenitence, nor at his refusing to acknowledge himself guilty of magic, both under torture and at his execution, for it is known that magicians promise the devil never to confess this crime, and he in return hardens their heart, so that they go to their death stupid and altogether insensible to their misfortunes." Before being put to the torture, the prisoner was addressed by Father Lactance, a man of great faith, chosen by the Bishop of Poitiers to exorcise the instruments of torture, as is always done in the case of magicians, in order to induce him to repent. Every one shed tears except the prisoner. M. de Laubardemont also spoke to him, together with the Lieutenant Criminel of Orleans, but, notwithstanding their efforts, they made no impression. This determined M. de Laubardemont to try the effects of torture. The boots[12] were applied, and the judge repeated his questions as to his accomplices. He always replied that he was no magician; though he had committed greater crimes than that. Questioned as to what crimes, he replied, crimes of human frailty, and added, that were he guilty of magic, he would be less ashamed of that than of his other crimes. This speech was ridiculous, especially in the mouth of a priest, who must know better than a layman that of all crimes the greatest is that of sorcery.

Torture drew from him nothing but cries, or rather sighs from the depth of his bosom, unaccompanied by tears, though the exorcist had abjured him, according to the ritual, to weep if he were innocent, but if guilty to remain tearless. Though he was very thirsty, he several times refused to drink holy water when presented to him. At length, pressed to drink, he took a few drops, with glaring eyes and a horrible look on his face. Never in the greatest agony of torture did he mention the name of Jesus Christ or of the Holy Virgin, save when repeating words he was ordered to speak, and then only in so cold a manner, and with such constraint, that he horrified the assistants. He never cast his eyes on the image of Christ, nor on that of the Virgin, which were opposite to him, and they were offered to him in vain: whereupon the judges remonstrated with him. They were still more scandalised when they tried to make him say the prayer which every good Christian addresses to his guardian angel, especially in great extremities, and he said he did not know it. Such was his conduct under torture: in such a crisis every feeling of religion would be awakened in an ordinary man.

His legs were then washed and placed near the fire to restore circulation; he then began to talk to the guards, joking and laughing, and would have gone on had they allowed him. He spoke neither of receiving the sacrament of penitence nor of imploring God's pardon. They had given him for a confessor Father Archangel, who asked him if he did not wish to confess. He replied that he had done so the previous Tuesday, after which he sat down and dined with the same appetite as usual, drank three or four glasses of wine, and spoke of all kinds of things except of God. Instead of listening to what was said to him for the good of his soul, he made speeches he had prepared beforehand as if he were preaching. They consisted in complaints as to the pain in his legs, and of a feeling of chilliness about his head, in asking for something to drink or to eat, and in begging that he might not be burnt alive.

When he was carried to the Court-house, where the Holy Fathers began to prepare him for death, he pushed back with his hand a crucifix which was presented to him, and muttered between his teeth some words which were not heard. His guards, witnessing this action, were scandalised, and told the monk not to offer him the crucifix again since he rejected it. He recommended himself to no one's prayers, neither before nor during the execution of the sentence—only, as he passed through the streets, turning his head on one side and the other to see the people, it was noticed that he said twice, with an appearance of vanity, "Pray God for me," and that those to whom he spoke were Huguenots, among whom was an Apostate. The monk who was with him exhorted him to say, "Cor mundum crea in me, Deus." Grandier turned his back on him and said with contempt, "Cor mundum crea in me, Deus."

Having reached the place of execution, the fathers redoubled their charitable solicitude, and pressed him most earnestly to be converted to God at that moment, offered him the crucifix, and placed it over his mouth and on his chest, he never deigned to look at it, and once or twice even turned away; he shook his head when holy water was offered him. He seemed eager to end his days, and in haste to have the fire lighted, either because he expected not to feel it, or because he feared he might be weak enough to name his accomplices; or perhaps, as is believed, in fear lest pain should extract from him a renunciation of his master Lucifer. For the devil, to whom magicians give themselves body and soul, so thoroughly masters their mind that they fear him only, and expect and hope for nothing save from him. Therefore did Grandier protest, placing his hand on his heart that he would say no more than he had already said. At last, seeing them set fire to the faggots, he feared they did not intend to keep their promise to him, but wished to burn him alive, and uttered loud complaints. The executioner then advanced, as is always done, to strangle him; but the flames suddenly sprang up with such violence that the rope caught fire, and he fell alive among the burning faggots. Just before this a strange event happened. In the midst of this mass of people, notwithstanding the noise of so many voices and the efforts of the archers who shook their halberts in the air to frighten them, a flight of pigeons flew round and round the stake. Grandier's partisans, impudent to the end, said that these innocent birds came, in default of men, as witnesses of his innocence; others thought very differently, and said that it was a troop of demons who came, as sometimes happens on the death of great magicians, to assist at that of Grandier, whose scandalous impenitence certainly deserved to be honoured in this manner. His friends, however, called this hardness of heart constancy, and had his ashes collected as if they were relics, they who did not believe in such things, for the Huguenots looked upon him as one of themselves, especially when they noticed that he never called on the Virgin nor looked on the crucifix.

Thus did he close his criminal career by a death which horrified not only Catholics, but even the more honourable of the Calvinist party.

But the end of the magician was not the end of the effects of his sorcery; and the possessions, far from ceasing, as had been hoped, continued for a time. God permitted that a great number of those who had been connected with the affair should be more or less vexed by demons. The Civil Lieutenant, Louis Chauvet, was seized with such fear that his mind gave way, and he never recovered. The Sieur Mannouri, the Surgeon who had sounded the marks[13] which the devil had impressed on the magician priest, suffering from extraordinary troubles, was of course said by the friends of Grandier to be the victim of remorse. Here are the particulars of the death of this Surgeon—

One night as he was returning about ten o'clock from visiting a sick man, walking with a friend, and accompanied by a man carrying a lantern, he cried all of a sudden, like a man awaking from a dream, "Ah! there is Grandier! what do you want?" At the same time he was seized with trembling. The two men took him back to his home, while he continued to talk to Grandier whom he thought he had before his eyes. He was put to bed filled with the same illusion, and shaking in every limb. He only lived a few days, during which his state never changed. He died believing the magician was still before him, and making efforts to keep him at arm's length.

Father Lactance, the worthy monk who had assisted the possessed in their sufferings, was himself attacked some time after the death of the priest. Feeling the first symptoms, he determined to go to Notre Dame des Ardilliers, whose chapel served by the priests of the oratory is held in great veneration in Saumur and its neighbourhood. M. de Canaye, who was going into the country, gave him a seat in his carriage. He had heard speak of his state, and knew that he was tormented by the devil, but he nevertheless joked about the matter, when, all of a sudden, whilst rolling along a perfectly level road, the carriage turned over with the wheels in the air without any one being in any way hurt. The next day they continued their voyage to Saumur when the carriage again turned over in the same way in the middle of the Rue du Faubourg de Fenet, which is perfectly smooth, and leads to the chapel of Ardillier. This holy monk afterwards experienced the greatest vexations from the demons, who at times deprived him of sight, and at times of memory; they produced in him violent fits of nausea, dulled his intelligence, and worried him in numerous ways. At length, after being tried by so many evils, God called him to Him.

Five years later, died of the same disease Father Tranquille. He was a holy monk, a celebrated preacher, gifted with a judicious mind, great piety, and a profound humility. A laborious exorcist, much feared by the devils, he had preferred that painful duty, generally little sought for, to the fame of preaching, and had devoted himself to the service of the possessed of Loudun. The demons, irritated at his constancy, determined to possess his body. But God never allowed him to be entirely possessed. Nevertheless, his cruel enemies succeeded in attacking his senses to a certain extent. They cast him to the ground, they cursed and swore out of his mouth, they caused him to put out his tongue and hiss like a serpent, they filled his mind with darkness, seemed to crush out his heart, and overwhelmed him with a thousand other torments.

On the day of Pentecoast they attacked him more violently than ever. He was to have preached, but was too ill to attempt it. But his confessor ordered the devil to leave him at liberty, and commanded the father to ascend the pulpit. He did so, and preached more eloquently than if he had prepared his sermon for weeks. This was his last sermon.

He performed mass for two or three days more, and then took to his bed to rise no more. The demons caused him pains, the violence of which none knew but he; they shrieked and howled out of his mouth, but he remained clear headed. The following morning the monks saw that God had given rein to the powers of hell, and had determined to abandon to them the life of the monk; and he himself begged that Extreme Unction should be administered to him when they should see that he was passing away. About twelve o'clock a demon who was being exorcised declared that Father Tranquille was at his last gasp. They hastened to see if it were true: he was dying, so the sacrament was administered to him. He died, and received the crown he had gained by combats with hell so courageously sustained.

The opinion of his holiness attracted an enormous crowd to his funeral. A Jesuit pronounced his funeral elogy, and a worthy epitaph was engraved on his tomb.

Another matter that should be mentioned is that when Extreme Unction was administered to him, the devils, driven away by the sacrament, were forced to leave him. But they did not go far; for they entered the body of another excellent monk who was present, and whom they possessed henceforward. They vexed him at first by violent contortions and horrible howlings, and at the moment of Tranquille's death they cried horribly, "He is dead;" as if they would say, "It is all over, no more hope of this soul!" At the same time, casting themselves on the other monk, they worked him so horribly that, in spite of the many that held him, he kept kicking in the most violent manner towards the deceased. He had to be carried away.

Father Surin, a Jesuit, had succeeded Father Lactance; he too had his trials.

The demons used to threaten him out of the mouth of the Mother Superior, who was under his care. Once, in the presence of the Bishop of Nimes, the demon took up his position on the face of the nun; suddenly he disappeared and attacked the father, made him grow pale, sat on his chest, and stopped his voice; but soon, obeying the order of another exorcist, he returned to the nun, spoke through her mouth, and showed himself extremely hideous and horrible on her face; and the father, returning to the fight, continued his duties as if he had never been attacked. In one afternoon he was thus attacked and released seven or eight times; but these assaults were followed by others still more violent, so that in his exorcisms he seemed to be struck with violent interior blows, borne to earth, and violently shaken by his adversary; he remained in this state sometimes half an hour, sometimes an hour. The other exorcists applied the Holy Sacrament to the places where he felt the demons, sometimes to his chest, sometimes to his head. When the devil left him he reappeared on the face of the mother, where the monk, with holy vengeance, pursued him, and constrained him to adore the Holy Sacrament. Once the devil threw him out of a window on to the rock where stands the convent of the Jesuits, and broke one of his thighs. After having sustained during many years with perfect patience and resignation these terrible trials, he was freed from them, and at length died in the odour of sanctity.

As to the Mother Superior, towards the end of the year 1635, something happened to her of a most extraordinary nature. Lord Montague came to Loudun, accompanied by two other English noblemen. He brought the exorcists a letter from the Archbishop of Tours, ordering them to edify his Lordship as much as possible. The Superior, in the midst of a convulsion, stretched out her left arm, and the name of Joseph appeared on it written in capital letters. The report of this event was signed by the English noblemen. Lord Montague hastened to Rome, abjured his heresy, embraced the ecclesiastical career, and, under another name, settled in France, where he lived many years. He is mentioned in the memoirs of Madame de Motteville.

At the beginning of 1636, on Twelfth Night, Father Surin resolved to compel the last demon that remained in the Mother Superior to adore Jesus Christ. He had the lady tied to a bench. The exorcisms drove the demon into a fury; and instead of obeying, he vomited a multitude of maledictions and blasphemies against the three persons of the Holy Trinity, against Jesus Christ, and against his Holy Mother, so execrable that one would be horrified to read them. The father knew that he was about to come out, and had the lady unbound. After tremblings, contortions, and horrible howlings, Father Surin pressed him more and more with the Holy Sacrament in his hand, and ordered him in Latin to write the name of Mary on the lady's hand. Raising her left arm into the air, the fiend redoubled his cries and howls, and in a last convulsion issued from the lady, leaving on her hand the holy name Maria, in letters so perfectly formed that no human hand could imitate them. The lady felt herself free and full of joy; and a *Te Deum* was sung in honour of the event.

Such is the true story of the possession of the nuns of Loudun and of the condemnation of Urbain Grandier, so different from the false accounts hitherto published. Even those who do not blush to deny the truth of infernal possessions need only notice that the human race has always believed, and still believes, that there are intelligent creatures in existence other than man, and almost similar to those whom the Pagans have always represented as Gods of Evil, or subterranean genii, like the demons believed in by Christians; and the belief in infernal possession, having in it no longer anything repugnant, will seem at once to them not only possible but probable. To believe that Urbain Grandier was unjustly condemned and executed, we must blindly believe hundreds of things which revolt common sense. One of the Protestant writers, for example, after having said in a thousand different ways that the possession of the nuns of Loudun was a mere imposture and horrible farce, confesses that it is impossible to conceive human beings, and especially women, driving a priest to a horrible death by such a series of feigned possessions.

FOOTNOTES:

12.   Boot or Bootikin, an instrument of judicial torture formerly used as a means of extorting confessions or evidence. It was originally brought from Russia, and consisted of a narrow wooden box made by nailing four planks together, and the leg of the prisoner being placed in it, wedges were inserted between the calf of the leg and the sides of the box, and struck home with a mallet. Sometimes a case of iron was used in a similar way, and occasionally the wedges were placed against the shin bone. The torture, which was of the most horrible character, was sometimes administered until the limbs were wholly crushed and rendered for ever useless. In the judicial records of Scotland there are many instances given of the application of the boot, and some of the details are of the most revolting character. It was last used in 1690, when an English gentleman named Neville Payne was, by the express command of William III., submitted to the torture of the thumb-screw and boot, and which in his case were applied with fearful severity. It is believed that all judicial torture had been given up in England about fifty years previous to this, and it was finally abolished by 7 Anne, c. 20.

13.   "There have been many found in whom such characters have concurred, as by the observation of all ages and nations, are symptoms of a witch; particularly the witch's marks, *mala fama*, inability to shed tears, etc., all of them providential discoveries of so dark a crime, and which, like avenues, lead us to the secret of it. 'Tis true, one man, through the concurrence of corrosive humours, may have an insensible mark, another may be enviously defamed, and a third, through sudden grief or melancholy, not be able to weep. One or other of these may concurr in the innocent, but none do attest that all of them have concurred in any one person but a witch; and 'tis reasonable to think that these indicia taking place in witches through all places in the world, do proceed from a common cause, rather than a peculiar humour. 'Tis but rational to think that the devil, aping God, should imprint a sacrament of his covenant; and it is thought by many, of greatest repute in the learned world, that whatsoever way, whether by accident or otherwise, such insensible marks be in the body, yet no such mark as theirs, every circumstance considered, is to be found with any other but themselves. I need not insist much in describing this mark, which is sometimes like a little teate, sometimes but a blewish spot; and I myself have seen it in the body of a confessing witch, like a little powder-mark, of a blea colour, somewhat hard, and withall insensible, so as it did not bleed when I pricked it."—*A Discourse of Witchcraft, by Mr. John Bell, Minister of the Gospel at Gladsmuir, 1705, MS.* [Quoted by T. D. Morison in his Edition of Sharpe's Witchcraft.]

In another printed Tract, by the same author, entitled, "The Trial of Witchcraft; or Witchcraft Arraigned and Condemned, in some answers to a few Questions anent Witches and Witchcraft, wherein is shewed how to know if one be a Witch, as also when one is bewitched: With some Observations upon the Witch's Mark, their compact with the Devil, the White Witches, &c."—he says, "The witch mark is sometimes like a blew spot, or a little teate, or reid spots, like flea biting; sometimes also the flesh is sunk in, and hollow, and this is put in secret places, as among the hair of the head, or eye-brows, within the lips, under the arm-pits, and even in the most secret parts of the body." Mr. Robert Kirk, minister at Aberfoill, in his Secret Commonwealth, describes the witch's mark—"A spot that I have seen, as a small mole, horny, and brown-coloured; throw which mark, when a large brass pin was thrust, (both in buttock, nose, and rooff of the mouth,) till it bowed and became crooked, the witches, both men and women, nather felt a pain nor did bleed, nor knew the precise time when this was doing to them, (their eyes only being covered)."

APPENDIX I.
The Duke of Lauderdale on Witchcraft

Instances sent me (Baxter) from the Duke of Lauderdale; more in other Letters of his I gave away, and some Books of Forreign Wonders he sent me.

Sir,

It is sad that the Sadducean, or rather atheistical denying of spirits, or their apparitions, should so far prevail; and sadder, that the clear testimonies of so many ancient and modern authors should not convince them. But why should I wonder, if those who believe not Moses and the prophets, will not believe though one should rise from the dead? One great cause of the hardening of these infidels is, the frequent impostures which the Romanists obtrude on the world in their exorcisms and pretended miracles. Another is the too great credulity of some who make everything witchcraft which they do not understand; and a third may be the ignorance of some judges and juries, who condemn silly melancholy people upon their own confession, and perhaps slender proofs. None of these three can be denied, but it is impertinent arguing to conclude, that because there have been cheats in the world, because there are some too credulous, and some have been put to death for witches, and were not, therefore all men are deceived. There is so much written, both at home and abroad, so convincingly, and by so unquestionable authors, that I have not the vanity to add any thing, especially to you;

but because you have desired me to tell you the story of the nuns at Loudun, and some others, I shall first tell you of a real possession near the place I was born in; next of disquietings by spirits, (both of which I had from unquestionable testimonies) and then I shall tell you what I saw at Loudun, concerning that which I do not doubt to call a pretended possession, sure I am a cheat. About 30 years ago, when I was a boy at school, there was a poor woman generally believed to be really possessed. She lived near the town of Duns, in the Mers, and Mr John Weems, then minister of Duns, (a man known by his works to be a learned man, and I knew him to be a godly honest man,) was perswaded she was possessed. I have heard him many times speak with my father about it, and both of them concluded it a real possession. Mr Weems visited her often, and being convinced of the truth of the thing, he, with some neighbour ministers, applied themselves to the king's privy council for a warrant to keep days of humiliation for her; but the bishops being then in power, would not allow any fasts to be kept. I will not trouble you with many circumstances; one I shall only tell you, which I think will evince a real possession. The report being spread in the country, a knight of the name of Forbes, who lived in the north of Scotland, being come to Edinborough, meeting there with a minister of the north, and both of them desirous to see the woman, the northern minister invited the knight to my father's house, (which was within ten or twelve miles of the woman) whither they came, and next morning went to see the woman. They found her a poor ignorant creature, and seeing nothing extraordinary, the minister says in Latin to the knight, "*Nondum audivimus spiritum loquentem.*" Presently a voice comes out of the woman's mouth, "*Audis loquentem, audis loquentem.*" This put the minister into some amazement, (which I think made him not mind his own Latin,) he took off his hat, and said, "*Misereatur Deus peccatoris;*" the voice presently out of the woman's mouth said, "*Dic peccatricis, dic peccatricis;*" whereupon both of them came out of the house fully satisfied, took horse immediately, and returned to my father's house at Thirlestoane Castle, in Lauderdale, where they related this passage. This I do exactly remember. Many more particulars might be got in that country, but this Latin criticism, in a most illiterate ignorant woman, where there was no pretence to dispossessing, is evidence enough, I think.

Within these 30 or 40 years, there was an unquestionable possession in the United Provinces; a wench that spoke all the languages, of which I have heard many particulars when I lived in the Low Countries. But that being forreign, I will not insist on it.

As to houses disquieted with noises, I shall tell you one that happened since I was a married man, and hint at more, which, if you please, I can get you authentically attested.

Within four miles of Edinborough, there lived an aged godly minister, one that was esteemed a Puritan; his son, now minister of the same place, and then ordained his assistant. Their house was extraordinarily troubled with noises, which they and their family, and many neighbours (who for divers weeks used to go watch with them) did ordinarily hear. It troubled them most on the Saturday night, and the night before their weekly lecture day. Sometimes they would hear all the locks in the house, on doors and chests, to fly open; yea, their cloaths, which were at night locked up into trunks and chests, they found in the morning all hanging about the walls. Once they found their best linnen taken out, the table covered with it, napkins as if they had been used, yea, and liquor in their cups as if company had been there at meat. The rumbling was extraordinary; the good old man commonly called his family to prayer when it was most troublesome, and immediately it was converted into gentle knocking, like the modest knock of a finger; but as soon as prayer was done, they should hear excessive knocking, as if a beam had been heaved by strength of many men against the floor. Never was there voice or apparition; but one thing was remarkable (you must know that it is ordinary in Scotland to have a half cannon-bullet in the chimney-corner, on which they break their great coals,) a merry maid in the house, being accustomed to the rumblings, and so her fear gone, told her fellow maid-servant that if the devil troubled them that night, she would brain him, so she took the half cannon-bullet into bed; the noise did not fail to awake her, nor did she fail in her design, but took up the great bullet, and with a threatning, threw it, as she thought, on the floor, but the bullet was never more seen; the minister turned her away for meddling and talking to it. All these particulars I have had from the mouth of the minister, now living; he is an honest man, of good natural parts, well bred both in learning and by travel into foreign parts in his youth. I was not in the country myself during the time, but I have it from many other witnesses; and my father's steward lived then in a house of mine, within a mile of the place, and sent his servants constantly thither; his son now serves me, who knows it.

I could tell you an ancienter story before my time, in the house of one Burnet, in the north of Scotland, where strange things were seen, which I can get sufficiently attested. Also in the southwest border of Scotland, in Annandale, there is a house called Powdine, belonging to a gentleman called Johnston; that house hath been haunted these 50 or 60 years. At my coming to Worcester, 1651, I spoke with the gentleman, (being myself quartered within two miles of the house,) he told me many extraordinary relations consisting in his own knowledge; and I carried him to my master, to whom he made the same relations,—noises and apparitions, drums and trumpets heard before the last war, yea, he said that some English soldiers quartered in his house were soundly beaten by that irresistible inhabitant; (this last I wondered at, for I rather expected he should have been a remonstrater, and opposed the resistance,) and within this fortnight Mr. James Sharp was with me, (him you know, and he is now at London,) he tells me that spirit now speaks, and appears frequently in the shape of a naked arm; but other discourses took me off from further inquiry. These things I tell you in obedience to your desire, but as I said before, I desire them not to be printed. Atheists are not to be convinced by stories; their own senses will no more convert them than sense will convert a papist from transubstantiation; and Scottish stories would make the disaffected jeer Scotland, which is the object of scorn enough already.

When I was in Dorsetshire, prisoner, one Mr Jo. Hodder, minister of Hauke-church, in that county, told me of strange apparitions and unquestionable evidences of the actings of spirits in a house, yea, a religious house of that county, of which he was himself an ear and eye-witness.

In Dorchester also, the son of a Reverend Mr Jo. White, (who was assessor to the Assembly at Westminster,) told me many particulars of that house in Lambeth, where his father lived in the time of the Assembly, which then was unquestionably haunted with spirits. I do well remember I dined with old Mr White there one day, and at dinner he told me much of it; and that that morning the spirit called up the maid to lay the beef to the fire. Of the two last you maybe satisfied when you please: and at this present I am told that there is a house at Folie-John-Park, not three miles from the place, haunted with spirits.

But I must leave room for my Loudun nuns, and not write a book. In the year 1637, being at Paris in the spring, the city was so full of the possession of a whole cloyster of nuns, and some laick wenches at Loudun, books printed, and strange stories told, that few doubted it; and I, who was perswaded such a thing might be, and that it was not impossible the devil could possess a nun as well as another, doubted it as little as any body. So coming into that country, I went a day's journey out of my way to satisfy my curiosity. Into the chappel I came in the morning of a holy day, and with as little prejudice as any could have, for I believed verily to have seen some strange sights; but when I had seen exorcising enough of three or four of them in the chappel, and could hear nothing but wanton wenches singing baudy songs in French, I began to suspect a fourbe, and in great gravity went to a jesuite, and told him I had come a great way in hope to see some strange thing, and was sorry to be disappointed. He commended my holy curiosity, and after he had thought a while, he desired me to go to the Castle, and from thence, at such an hour, to the parish church, and I should be satisfied. I wondered at his correspondence, yet gravely went where he directed me. In the Castle I saw little, but in the parish church I saw a great many people gazing, and a wench pretty well taught to play tricks, yet nothing so much as I have seen twenty tumblers and rope-dancers do. Back I came to the nuns chappel, where I saw the Jesuits still hard at work, at several altars, and one poor capuchin, who was an object of pity, for he was possessed indeed with a melancholy fancy that devils were running about his head, and constantly was applying relicks. I saw the mother superior exorcised, and saw the hand on which they would have made us believe the names I. H. S. Maria Joseph were written by miracles; (but it was apparent to me it was done with aquafortis) then my patience was quite spent, and I went to a Jesuit and told him my mind freely. He still maintained a real possession, and I desired for a tryal, to speak a strange language. He asked, "What language?" I told him, "I would not tell; but neither he nor all those devils should understand me." He asked, "If I would be converted upon the tryal?" (for I had discovered I was no papist.) I told him, "That was not the question, nor could all the devils in hell pervert me; but the question was, if that was a real possession, and if any could understand me, I shall confess it under my hand." His answer was, "These devils have not travelled;" and this I replied to with a loud laughter, nor could I get any more satisfaction; only in the town I heard enough that it was a cheat invented to burn a curate, (his name, as I take it, was Cupiff,) and the man had been really burned to ashes as a witch, but the people said it was for his conversion from them. At my coming to Saumar next day, my countryman, Dr. Duncan, Principle of the

College at Saumar, told me how he had made a clearer discovery of the cheat in presence of the Bishop of Poitiers, and of all the country, how he had held fast one of the pretended nuns arms, in spite of all the power of their exorcisms, and challenged all the devils in hell to take it out of his hand. This, with many more circumstances, he told me, and he printed them to the world; but this is already too tedious. One more journey I made to see possessed women exorcised near Antwerp, anno 1649; but saw only some great Holland wenches hear exorcism patiently, and belch most abominably. So if those were devils, they were windy devils, but I thought they were only possessed with a morning's draught of too new beer. Some of the Loudun nuns, after great resistance and squeeking, did, on great importunity, adore their host, and the jesuites did desire us to see the power of the church, where all I wondered at was his blasphemy, in saying to the pretended devil,—"*Prostratum adorabis creatorem tuum, quem digitis teneo*;" but my paper, as well as my discretion, calls for an end. Your desire, and my obedience, is all I can plead for your receiving so long a rabble, from, Sir,

Your most faithful Friend and Servant,
Lauderdaile.
Windsor Castle, March 12, 1659.

APPENDIX II.

[The following Notes are taken from Arnot's Collection of Criminal Trials in Scotland]:—

1588.

Alison Pearson.

Alison Pearson in Byre-hills, Fifeshire,[14] was convicted of practising sorcery, and of invoking the Devil. She confessed that she had associated with the Queen of the Fairies for many years,[15] and that she had friends in the Court of Elfland, who were of her own blood. She said that William Simpson, late the King's smith, was, in the eighth year of his age, carried off by an Egyptian to Egypt, where he remained twelve years; and that this Egyptian was a giant: That the Devil appeared to her in the form of this William Simpson, who was a great scholar, and a doctor of medicine, who cured her diseases: That he has appeared to her, accompanied with many men and women, who made merry with bag-pipes, good cheer, and wine: That the good neighbours [16] attended, and prepared their charms in pans over the fire; that the herbs of which they composed their charms, were gathered before sunrise; and that with these they cured the Bishop of St. Andrews of a fever and flux.—She underwent all the legal forms customary in cases of witchcraft, *i.e.* she was convicted and condemned, strangled and burned.

1590.

Janet Grant and Janet Clerk.

Janet Grant and Janet Clerk [17] were convicted of bewitching several persons to death, of taking away the privy members of some folks, and bestowing them on others; and of raising the devil.

John Cunninghame.

It was proved against John Cunninghame, that the Devil appeared to him in white raiment,[18] and promised, that, if he would become his servant, he should never want, and should be revenged of all his enemies: That he was carried in an ecstacy to the kirk of North Berwick, where the Devil preached to him, and many others, bidding them not spare to do evil, but to eat, drink, and be merry; for he should raise them all up gloriously at the Last Day: That the Devil made him do homage, by kissing his.... That he (the prisoner) raised the wind on the King's passage to Denmark: That he met with Satan on the King's return from Denmark; and Satan promised to raise a mist by which his Majesty should be thrown upon the coast of England; and thereupon threw something like a football into the sea, which raised a vapour.

Agnes Sampson.

Agnes Sampson in Keith,[19] a grave matron-like woman, of a rank and comprehension above the vulgar, was accused of having renounced her baptism, and of having received the devil's mark; of raising storms to prevent the Queen's coming from Denmark; of being at the famous meeting at North Berwick, where six men and ninety women, witches, were present, dancing to one of their number, who played to them on a Jew's-harp. It was charged in the indictment that the Devil was present at this meeting; and started up in the pulpit, which was hung round with black candles: That he called them all by their names, asked them, If they had kept their promises, and been good servants, and what they had done since the last meeting: That they opened up three graves, and cut off the joints from the dead bodies fingers, and that the prisoner got for her share two joints and a winding sheet, to make powder of to do mischief: That the Devil was dressed in a black gown and hat; and that he ordered them to keep his commandments, which were to do all the ill they could, and to kiss his....

1591.

Euphan M'Calzeane.

Euphan M'Calzeane was a lady possessed of a considerable estate in her own right. She was the daughter of Thomas M'Calzeane Lord Cliftonhall, one of the Senators of the College of Justice, whose death in the year 1581, spared him the disgrace and misery of seeing his daughter fall by the hands of the executioner. She was married to a gentleman of her own name, by whom she had three children. She was accused of treasonably conspiring the King's death by enchantments;[20] particularly by training a waxen picture of the King; of raising storms to hinder his return from Denmark; and of various other articles of witchcraft. She was heard by counsel in her defence; was found guilty by the jury, which consisted of landed gentlemen of note; and her punishment was still severer than that commonly inflicted on the Weyward Sisters,—She was burned alive, and her estate confiscated. Her children, however, after being thus barbarously robbed of their mother, were [21] restored by act of Parliament against the forfeiture. The act does not say that the sentence was unjust; but that the King was touched in honour and conscience to restore the children. But to move the wheels of his Majesty's conscience, the children had to grease them, by a payment of five thousand merks to the donator of escheat,[22] and by relinquishing the estate of Clifton-hall, which the King gave to Sir James Sandilands of Slamanno.

As a striking picture of the state of justice, humanity, and science in those times,[23] it may be remarked that this Sir James Sandilands, a favourite of the King's, ("ex interiore principis familiaritate,") who got this estate, which the daughter of one Lord of Session forfeited, on account of being a witch, did that very year murder another Lord of Session in the suburbs of Edinburgh, in the public street, without undergoing either trial or punishment.

1620.

Margaret Wallace.

Margaret Wallace [24] was tried before the Court of Justiciary. The Duke of Lennox, the Archbishop of Glasgow, and Sir George Erskine of Innerteil, sat as assessors to the judges, and an eminent counsel was heard in behalf of the prisoner. She was accused of inflicting and of curing diseases by inchantment; but it was not specified what spells she employed. It was libelled against her, that on being taken suddenly ill she sent for one Christian Graham, a notorious witch, who afterwards suffered a capital punishment, and that this witch transferred the disease from the prisoner to a young girl: That the girl being thus taken ill, her mother was advised by the prisoner to send for Christian Graham, who answered, that her confidence was in God, and she would have nothing to do with the Devil or his instruments: The prisoner replied, "That in a case of this sort Christian Graham could do as much as God himself; and that without her aid there was no remedy for the child:" But the mother not consenting, the prisoner without her knowledge sent for Christian, who muttered words, and expressed signs, by which she restored the child to health, &c. Her counsel urged, that the indictment was much too general: That it ought to have been specified, not simply that she did enchant, but also by what kind of spells she performed her incantations: That supposing Christian Graham to have been a witch, and that the prisoner when taken ill consulted her, still he was entitled to plead that the prisoner consulted her on account of her medical knowledge, and not for her skill in sorcery: That as to blasphemous expressions however well they might found a trial for blasphemy, they by no means inferred the crime of witchcraft; and he quoted many authorities from the Civil and Canon laws. He farther challenged one of the assizers, because one of the articles charged against the prisoner was her having done an injury to his brother-in-law.—The whole defences were repelled by the judges; and the jury found the prisoner guilty.

1629.
Isobel Young.

Isobel Young in East Barns was accused of having stopped by enchantment George Sandie's mill twenty-nine years before; of having prevented his boat from catching fish while all the other boats at the herring-drave, or herring fishery, were successful; and that she was the cause of his failing in his circumstances, and of nothing prospering with him in the world: That she threatened mischief against one Kerse, who thereupon lost the power of his leg and arm: That she entertained several witches in her house, one of whom went out at the roof in likeness of a cat, and then resumed her own shape: That she took a disease off her husband, laid it under the barn floor, and transferred it to his nephew, who when he came into the barn saw the firlot hopping up and down the floor: That she used the following charm to preserve herself and her cattle from an infectious distemper, viz. to bury a white ox and a cat alive throwing in a quantity of salt along with them: That she had the Devil's mark, &c.

Mr Laurence Macgill and Mr David Primrose appeared as counsel for the prisoner. They pleaded, that the mill might have stopped, the boat catched no fish, and the man not prospered in the world, from—natural causes; and it was not libelled by what spells she had accomplished them: That as to the man who had lost the power of his leg and arm, first, she never had the least acquaintance with him; secondly, she offered to prove that he was lame previous to the threatening expressions which she was said to have used: That the charge of laying a disease under a barn floor was a ridiculous fable, taken probably from a similar story in Ariosto; and that two years had elapsed between her husband's illness and his nephew's: That what the prosecutor called the Devil's mark was nothing else than the scar of an old ulcer; and that the charge of her burying the white ox and the cat was false.

The celebrated Sir Thomas Hope, who was counsel for the prosecution, replied, that these defences ought to be repelled, and no proof allowed of them, because contrary to the libel; that is to say, in other words, because what was urged by the prisoner in her defences contradicted what was charged by the public prosecutor in his indictment.—The defences for the prisoner were overruled.—Is it needful for me to add that she was convicted, strangled, and burned?

FOOTNOTES:
14.   Rec. of Just. 18th May 1588.
15.   In the original it is Queen of Elfland.
16.   Good Neighbours was a term for witches. People were afraid to speak of them oppro-briously, lest they should provoke their resentment.
17.   Records of Justiciary, 7th August 1590.
18.   Ibid, 26th December 1590.
19.   Rec. of Just. Jan. 27. 1590. A story is told of this woman in Spottiswood's Hist. p. 383. which is nowise confirmed by the record. His fable is absurd; and seems to have been invented by some zealous believer in the divine right of Kings.
20.   Rec. of Just., 8th May 1591.
21.   Unprinted Acts, A.D. 1592. No. 70.
22.   He who obtains a gift of the forfeiture.

23.   "Johnstoni Historia Rerum Britannicarum," p. 172.
24.   Records of Justiciary, March 20. 1620.

THE END.

About Grandier

VAMzzz Publishing

The fatal
friction
between a
womanizing
priest and
jealous nuns
possessed
by sex
demons...

Urbain Grandier

Urbain Grandier (born 1590 in Bouère – died 18 August 1634 in Loudun) was a French Catholic priest who was burned at the stake after being convicted of witchcraft, following the events of the Loudun Possessions. Urbain Grandier was appointed parish priest of St-Pierre-du-Marché in Loudun, a town in Poitou, France, in 1617. He was considered to be a very good-looking man, and was both wealthy and well-educated. This combination made the priest a target for the attention of girls in Loudun, including the nuns. Ignoring his vow of celibacy, he is known to have had sexual relationships with a number of women and to have acquired a reputation as a philanderer, leaving a trail of jealous women behind with dangerous loose ends. He also wrote a book attacking the discipline of clerical celibacy.

Modern commentators like Aldous Huxley, whose novel *The Devils of Loudun* (1952) is more famous than the book you are holding in your hands, have argued that the accusations began after Grandier refused to become the spiritual director of the convent, unaware that the Mother Superior, Sister Jeanne of the Angels, had become obsessed with him, having seen him from afar and heard of his sexual exploits. According to Huxley, Sister Jeanne, enraged by his rejection, instead invited Canon Mignon, an enemy of Grandier, to become the director. Jeanne then accused Grandier of using black magic to seduce her. The other nuns gradually began to make similar accusations. Grandier was interrogated and tried by an ecclesiastical tribunal, but Grandier was a very well-connected man, high in political circles. When he was arrested and found guilty of immorality on June 2, 1630, it was these connections that restored him to full clerical duties within the same year. However, Grandier had gained the enmity of the powerful Cardinal Richelieu, the chief minister of France, after a public verbal attack against him. Grandier had also written and published scathing criticisms of Richelieu.

Richelieu ordered a new trial, conducted by his special envoy Jean de Laubardemont, a relative of the Mother Superior of the convent of Loudun. Grandier was rearrested at Angers and the possibility of appealing to the Parlement of Paris was denied to him. Interrogated for a second time, the nuns (including the Mother Superior) did not renew their accusations, but this did not affect the predetermined outcome of the trial. While the defense witnesses were forced to flee, 72 witnesses swore evidence against Grandier, who was denied the normal procedure of trial by a secular court. Had he been tried by secular court, Grandier could have appealed to the Parliament of Paris. Instead, Richelieu's committee took charge of the legal proceedings. After torturing Father Grandier,

'Grandier also wrote a book attacking the discipline of clerical celibacy.'

the judges (clerics Lactance, Laubardemont, Surin and Tranquille) introduced documents purportedly signed by Grandier and several demons, as evidence that he had made a diabolical pact. It is unknown whether Grandier wrote or signed the pacts under duress, or whether they were entirely forged. Grandier was found guilty and sentenced to death. Despite the fact he had to endure the most horrible forms of torture, Grandier never confessed to witchcraft. He was burned alive at the stake. ■

Urbain Grandier burned alive in Loudun, after being accused of witchcraft, 1634, credited to Caspar Luyken, 1701

The exorcisms at Loudun

'For they were seventeen in number; and everyone was found to be either fully possessed, or partially under the influence of the Evil One.'

The text of this book reports severe cases of demonic possession:
'...they threw themselves back till their heads touched their feet, and walked in this position with wonderful rapidity, and for a long time. They uttered: cries so horrible and so loud that nothing like it was ever heard before; they made use of expressions so indecent as to shame the most debauched of men, while their acts, both in exposing themselves and inviting lewd behaviour from those present, would have astonished the inmates of the lowest brothel in the country;...'

Fathers Mignon and Barré performed exorcisms. Several of the nuns, including Jeanne des Anges, suffered violent convulsions during the procedure, shrieking and making sexual motions toward the priests. Following the lead of Jeanne des Anges, many of the nuns reported illicit dreams. The accusers would suddenly bark, scream, blaspheme, and contort their bodies. During the exorcisms, Jeanne swore that she and the other nuns were possessed by two demons named Asmodeus and Zebulun. These demons were sent to the nuns when Father Grandier tossed a bouquet of roses over the convent walls. The demon Gressil is mentioned for the first time in literature in the records of the Loudon possessions. Sebastien Michaelis would later assign Gressil the status of the demon of impurity and uncleanliness, third in the order of Thrones.

When exorcisms resumed at Loudun, they were led by the expert exorcists Capuchin Father Tranquille, Franciscan Father Lactance, and Jesuit Father Jean-Joseph Surin, and they were held publicly; up to 7,000 spectators attended. The priests employed dramatic commands, threats, and rituals to both direct and encourage the nuns in their accusations against Grandier. Adding to the hysteria prompted by the public exorcisms were the stories told by both nuns and Father Grandier's former lovers. As in both the Louviers possessions and the Aix-en-Provence possessions, the claims made against Grandier were overtly sexual and showed visible physical responses. Because they were public and dramatic, it was an easy job to make Urbain Grandier a scapegoat for the citizens of Loudun and surrounding areas.

In addition to the dreams that Jeanne des Anges and other nuns had related, Jeanne added a third demon to the array of possessors afflicting the nuns: Isacaron, the devil of debauchery. After admitting to this third demon possessor, Jeanne went through a psychosomatic pregnancy. In all, Jeanne and the other nuns claimed to be possessed by a multitude of demons: Asmodeus, Zabulon, Isacaaron, Astaroth, Gresil, Amand, Leviatom, Behemot, Beherie, Easas, Celsus, Acaos, Cedon, Naphthalim, Cham, Ureil and Achas.

In a last effort to clear his name, Father Grandier performed an exorcism on the nuns himself. He spoke to the nuns in Greek, testing their knowledge of languages previously unknown to them (a sure sign of possession). The nuns had been coached, and responded that they had been ordered in their pact to never use Greek.

In another exorcism, performed by Father Gault, the priest obtained a promise from the demon Asmodeus to leave one of the nuns he was possessing. Later, a devil's pact allegedly written, between the Devil and Grandier was presented to the court. This pact, stolen from Lucifer's cabinet of pacts by Asmodeus himself, was signed in blood by Grandier and various demons. Asmodeus had apparently written out the same promise he'd given to Father Gault on this pact:
'I promise that when leaving this creature, I will make a slit below her heart as long as a pin, that this slit will pierce her shirt, bodice and cloth which will be bloody. And tomorrow, on the twentieth of May at five in the afternoon of Saturday, I promise that the demons Gresil and Amand will make their opening in the same way, but a little smaller - and I approve the promises made by Leviatam, Behemot, Beherie

'In a last effort to clear his name, Father Grandier performed an exorcism on the nuns himself.'

with their companions to sign, when leaving,
the register of the church of St. Croix! Given the
nineteenth of May 1629.'
Later historians would prove that this note was
written in Jeanne des Anges' hand. (See next,
The alleged Pact.)

Father Grandier was promised that he could
have the chance to speak before he was
executed, making a last statement, and that
he would be hanged before the burning, an
act of mercy. From the scaffold Grandier
attempted to address the crowd, but the
monks threw large quantities of holy water
in his face so that his last words could not be
heard. Then, according to historian Robert
Rapley, exorcist Lactance caused the execution
to deviate from the planned course of
action—enraged by taunting from the crowd
that gathered for the execution, Lactance lit
the funeral pyre before Grandier could be
hanged, leaving him to be burned alive.

The possessions failed to stop after Father
Grandier's execution; as a result, public
exorcisms continued. In his summary of the
Loudun possessions, author Moshe Sluhovsky
reports that these displays continued until
1637, three years after Grandier's death.
The last departing demons left clear signs of
their exit from Jeanne des Anges, the mother
superior of the community body, when
the names Joseph and Mary miraculously
appeared inscribed on des Anges's left arm. ■

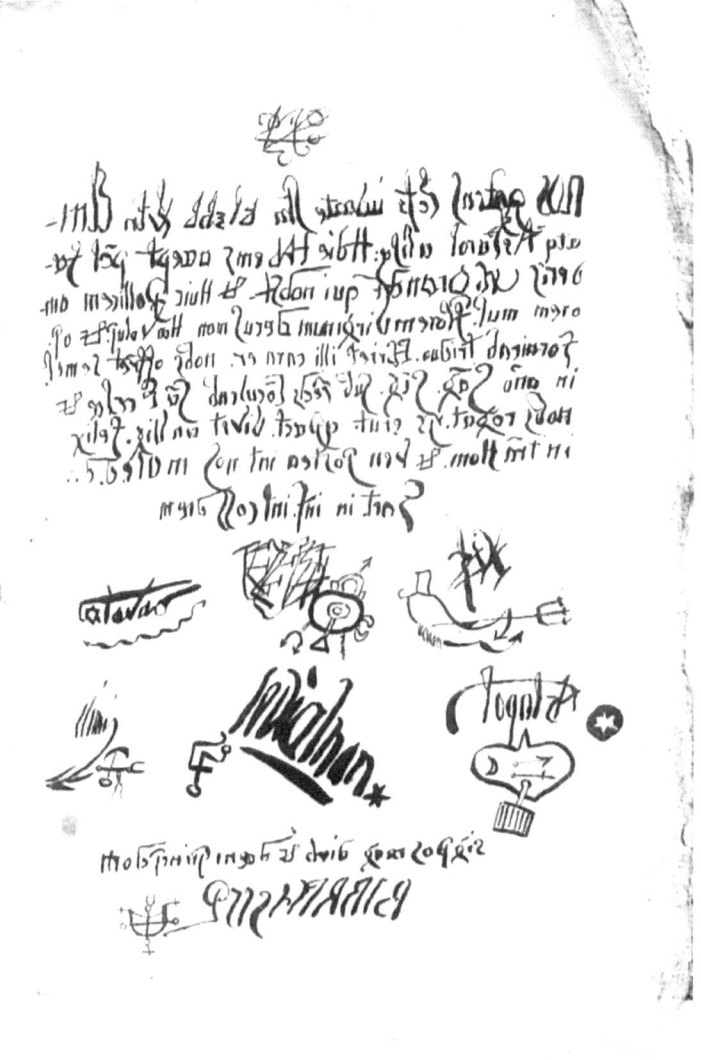

The alleged pact Grandier would have made with demons. Interestingly the sigil left below, looks very much like the sigil of Sitri, one of the entities (No 12) mentioned in the Goetia. According to the Goetia-text Sitri inflames the opposite sex with love and sexual desire and makes them want to expose themselves naked.

The Alleged Pact

Translation of the alleged pact of Urbain
Grandier with devils:

*We, the influential Lucifer, the young Satan,
Beelzebub, Leviathan, Elimi, and Astaroth,
together with others, have today accepted the
covenant pact of Urbain Grandier, who is ours.*

*And him do we promise the love of women,
the flower of virgins, the respect of monarchs,
honours, lusts and powers.*

*He will go whoring three days long; the carousal
will be dear to him. He offers us once in the year
a seal of blood, under the feet, he will trample
the holy things of the church and he will ask
us many questions; with this pact he will live
twenty years happy on the earth of men, and
will later join us to sin against God.*

Bound in hell, in the council of demons.
Lucifer Beelzebub Satan
Astaroth Leviathan Elimi
*The seals placed the Devil, the master, and the
demons, princes of the lord.*
Baalberith, writer.

The pact was allegedly signed by Urbain
Grandier and stolen from the Devil's cabinet
of pacts by the demon Asmodeus. This
pact shows the signatures of all demons in
possession of the Ursuline nuns at Loudun. ■

Paper books

VAMzzz Publishing

VAMzzz Publishing is located in the very centre of old Amsterdam, in The Netherlands. Our publishing company creates high quality revised editions of five star occult, witchcraft, Gothic and esoteric classics, mostly written in the Fin de siècle-period and early 20th century.

As a publisher, we deeply respect the writer of any book we choose, so we join our forces (top level graphic design & thirty years of occult studies) to produce enchanting volumes which maximize the reading pleasure and inform, often with extra added information. In contrast to the current trend of digital screen addiction, we think, this variety of literature needs to be presented on paper. *No e-books, but real books!*

Apart from re-publications of valuable but forgotten books, we are also in the preparation of new publications on topics such as self-healing, magic, new astrology and more.

Previews of all books including a complete table of contents can be viewed on www.vamzzz.com. More books will be added to the list. Please visit our website regularly for the latest updates.

VAMzzz Publishing
P.O. Box 3340
1001 AC Amsterdam
The Netherlands
contactvamzzz@gmail.com
www.vamzzz.com

FREE MAGAZINE BY VAMZZZ.COM   0116

PAN
PURE MAGIC

OCCULT
Basque Witchcraft

MAGICAL NATURE
The Poppy

GHOST STORY
The Empty House

ASTROLOGY
& Money Magic

PAGANISM
Hekate Ritual

ART
Salvator Rosa

VAMZZZ PUBLISHING
Demonology and Devil-Lore

Recommended

PAN Magazine
by VAMzzz Publishing
Free Online
www.vamzzz.com/pan.html

In Greek religion and mythology, PAN, the companion of the nymphs, is the god of the wild, shepherds and flocks, wild mountains and rustic music. He has the hindquarters, legs and horns of a goat, in the same manner as a faun or satyr. He is also recognized as the god of fields, groves and wooded glens; connected to fertility, the joy of life itself and the season of spring.

Though a mortal god in antiquity and an underground witch-god in medieval times, the last decades PAN has become a patron of both modern occultism, Wicca, paganism and the green guerilla – enthroned again as the one and only God of the Earth and Nature. PAN is the vibe touching those who refuse to become part of a machine, and who remain loyal to Mother Nature, the visible and hidden one. Therefore PAN is the most suitable icon we could chose for this periodical.

The Banshee
A Ghost Hunter's Investigation
by Elliot O'Donnell
222 pages, Paperback, ISBN 9789492355232

The banshee is a mysterious female spirit in Irish folklore, who heralds the death of a family member, usually by shrieking or keening. The screeching sound is described as somewhere between the wail of a woman and the moan of an owl, a low singing or piercing loud and able to break glass. The banshee appears as an old hag or beautiful lady, but may also appear as a crow, stoat, hare and weasel - animals associated in Ireland with witchcraft.

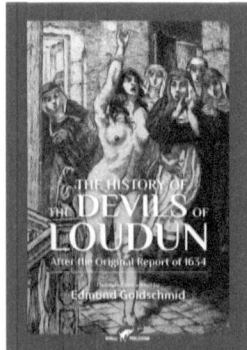

The History of the Devils of Loudun
After the Original Report of 1634
Translation by Edmund Goldschmid
118 pages, Paperback, ISBN 9789492355256

Around 1632 seventeen Ursuline Nuns were taken over by demons and went into a sexual and blasphemous state of hysteria for years. The work also describes the trial of a womanizing local priest named Father Urbain Grandier, who was accused of summoning these demons and, in the end, burned at the stake.

Religion and Lust
or The Physical Correlation of Religious Emotion and Sexual Desire
by James Weir Jr.
146 pages, Paperback, ISBN 9789492355270

In *Religion and Lust*, author James Weir Jr. investigates the origins of religious feeling, the once world wide spread fertility worship and the physical correlation of religious emotion and sexual desire. A major part of the work is filled with a colourful collection of religious or semi-religious, sexual rites, once practiced all over the globe, connecting the most "primitive" tribe to the most "civilized" nations.

Incubi and Succubi or Demoniality
A Historical Study of Sexual Contacts with Demons
by Sinistrari of Ameno
194 pages, Paperback, ISBN 9789492355263

This book is a revised English edition of Sinistrari's fascinating 17th century study on the orgasm-stimulating sex demon. The incubus and succubus are the same creature. The incubus is its male shape, copulates with women. The succubus visits men, triggering wet dreams. The intercourse with this astral visitor was called demoniality, a term no longer in use, though nowadays people are still having these mysterious incubus/succubus-"sexperiences".

Mysteria
History of the Secret Doctrines & Mystic Rites of Ancient Religions & Medieval and Modern Secret Orders
by Dr. Otto Henne am Rhyn
288 pages, Paperback, ISBN 9789492355225

Mysteria is a treasure box of missing conspiracy links and one of the very few publications, which offer reliable information about Adam Weishaupt's Illuminati for "the web & media-disinformed". Lodge-insider Otto Henne am Rhyn takes you on a journey, back to the Mystery cults of ancient Egypt, Babylon and Greece, passes Templars and explains modern lodges.

Magic and Magical Fetish
by Alfred Cort Haddon
108 pages, Paperback, ISBN 9789492355300

Alfred C. Haddon gives a practical and theoretical insight of the universal principles of magic, categorized in different techniques. The book is one of the very few works ever published, which describes wind and rain making. Magic is divided into sympathetic magic, the magic of words, talismans and divination, magical training routines. A kaleidoscope of forgotten magical techniques, which wasn't available for decades.

The Eleusian and Bacchic Mysteries
A Dissertation
by Thomas Taylor
200 pages, Paperback, ISBN 9789492355294

The Eleusian and Bacchic Mysteries focus on life, death and rebirth in a living nature (the present), while this nature was regarded as the converging of past and future. Taylor describes a series of lost secret rites. These rites were once the appointed means for regeneration through an inner union with the Divine Essence, despite their wild and sexual aspect.

Numbers
Their Occult Power and Mystic Virtues
by W. Wynn Westcott
170 pages, Paperback, ISBN 9789492355287

This book may be regarded as the "bible of numerology". It deals with Pythagorean number divisions, explains 3 different kinds of Kabalistic numerology, and reveals the hidden logic and symbolism of the numbers 1,2,3,4,5,6,7,8,9,10,11,12 and 13. This is accompanied by a long course of numbers between 14 and 25920. Special symbolisms are included like the link between numbers and planets and numbers in relation to the Apocalypse.

Sorceress
A Study of Witches and their Relations with Demons
by Jules Michelet
432 pages, Paperback, ISBN 9789492355249

This work is one of the most vivid, dark and confronting studies on witchcraft ever produced. Long before Murray's Witch-Cult in Western Europe, Michelet positions the medieval witch within a diminishing ancient culture of nature worship and the ruthless efforts of Christianity, with its cruel hostility towards nature, life (and women), to overwrite it. A nightmare of the most extraordinary verisimilitude and poetical power...

Aradia
Gospel of the Witches
by Charles Godfrey Leland
174 pages, Paperback, ISBN 9789492355010

This wonderful book describes the creation according to Italian witch-lore. We also read about the witch-meeting or sabbath (treguenda) and the book contains many original magical recipes, like spells for love and good fortune. Diana is further connected to the Moon and the fairy world.

Demonology and Devil-Lore (Volume 1)
by Moncure Daniel Conway
490 pages, Paperback, ISBN 9789492355157

Demonology and Devil-Lore (Volume 2)
by Moncure Daniel Conway
518 pages, Paperback, ISBN 9789492355164

Within the demonology scope, this rare and mostly forgotten, almost 1000 pages thick masterpiece, remains unsurpassed in quality and completeness. Even in the 21st century the works offer fascinating missing links for both the academic and student of occult traditions. Moncure Daniel Conway divides Volume 1 in three parts and deals mainly with the evolution and thematic classification of ex-gods, demons and nature creatures. Volume 2 deals primarily with the diabolic and with the Devil himself, his ethnic history and connected topics.

Fairy Mythology *(Volume 1)*
Romance and Superstition of Various Countries 1
by Thomas Keightley
404 pages, Paperback, ISBN 9789492355096

Fairy Mythology *(Volume 2)*
Romance and Superstition of Various Countries 2
by Thomas Keightley
404 pages, Paperback, ISBN 9789492355102

The term Fairy covers all kinds of nature spirits, not just the tiny sugarsweet creatures hovering around flowers. A unique and impressive book on this subject, published in a revised 2 volume-edition. No wiccan or pagan can afford to leave these books unopened. About Elves, Dwarfs, Kobolds, Trolls, Changelings, Meremaids, Nisses, Fairies, Brownies, Puck and other Elemental spirits all over the world.

Etruscan Magic & Occult Remedies
(Two volumes in one book)
by Charles Godfrey Leland
628 pages, Paperback, ISBN 9789492355003

Part One of the book gives us a complete and detailed insight in the Etruscan and Roman rooted pantheon of the Tuscan Streghe (witches). Part Two describes many of their spells, incantations, sorcery and several lost divination methods. Much information in this book, Leland received first hand from the Tuscan witches Maddalena and Marietta.

Voodoos and Obeahs
Phases of West India Witchcraft
by Joseph J. Williams
374 pages, Paperback, ISBN 9789492355119

This work goes into great depth concerning the New World-African connection and is highly recommended if you want a deep understanding of the dramatic historical background of Haitian and Jamaican magic and witchcraft, and the profound influence of imperialism, slavery and racism on its development. Williams includes numerous quotations from rare documents and books on the topic.

Devil-worship in France
Or The Question of Lucifer
by Arthur Edward Waite
240 pages, Paperback, ISBN 9789492355065

In *Devil-Worship in France,* Waite attempts to discern what is genuine from what is fake in the evidence of 19th century Satanism. To get the answers he spends a great deal of time investigating the French Masonic echelon, debunking a "conspiracy of falsehood" and determining what should be understood by Satanism and what not. Huysmans' diabolical novel *Là-Bas* (1891) inspired Waite to write this sceptical analysis.

Testament of Solomon
A First Century AD Grimoire
76 pages, Paperback, ISBN 9789492355041

A first century AD grimoire, and therefore the oldest, and least known, of all grimoires (magical instruction books) in the occult tradition. The book describes health inflicting demons of zodiacal decans, summoned by King Solomon, and how he controlled them to use their forces to build his temple and more. Translated by F. C. Conybeare, appeared first in the *Jewish Quarterly Review* of October, 1898.

Ophiolatreia
Rites and Mysteries of Serpent Worship
by Hargrave Jennings
186 pages, Paperback, ISBN 9789492355126

An account of the rites and mysteries connected with the origin, rise and development of serpent worship in various parts of the world, enriched with interesting traditions, and a full description of the celebrated serpent mounds & temples, the whole forming an exposition of one of the phases of phallic, or sex worship.

Anansi
Jamaican stories of the Spider God
by Martha Warren Beckwith
494 pages, Paperback, ISBN 9789492355171

Anansi is both a god, spirit and African folktale character. He often takes the shape of a spider and is considered to be the spirit of all knowledge of stories. He is also one of the most important characters of West African and Caribbean folklore.

Spiritual Fetichism
A Study of West African Culture, Witchcraft, Magic & Demonology
by Robert Hamill Nassau
524 pages, Paperback, ISBN 9789492355188

Despite a nowadays anachronist and disturbing perspective, the book has remained most valuable for students of the occult, especially those interested in demonology, voodoo, hoodoo and its roots, African magick and religion, witchcraft, the classes of African spirits, and of course the spiritual and magickal use of a fetish.

Là-Bas
A Journey into the Self
by Joris-Karl Huysmans
378 pages, Paperback, ISBN 9789492355058

The plot of *Là-Bas* concerns the novelist Durtal, who is disgusted by the emptiness and vulgarity of the modern world. He seeks relief by turning to the study of the Middle Ages. Through his contacts in Paris, Durtal discovers that Satanism is not a thing of the past but alive and kicking in turn of the century France. The novel culminates with a description of a black mass.

Unicorn
A mythological investigation
by Robert Brown Jr.
124 pages, Paperback, ISBN 9789492355072

Brown Jr. believes the unicorn to be a lunar symbol, and draws on mythology from a wide range of sources all over the world to build his case. The author discusses the heraldic use of the unicorn, relates the creature to ancient goddesses like Astarte, Hecate en the Gorgon Medusa, and provides the reader with lost esoteric Moon-lore.

The House of Souls
A Fragment of Life / The White People
The Great God Pan / The Inmost Light
by Arthur Machen
336 pages, Paperback, ISBN 9789492355218

A collection of four masterpieces of horror and mystery, first collectively published in 1906. In the ingenious plot of *The Great God Pan,* a young woman is forced into Pan's reality, and turns into a femme fatale. *The Inmost Light* involves a doctor's scientific experiments into occultism and a vampiric force. In *The White People* a young girl's diary is discovered, describing her initiation into a secret world of folklore and ritual magic. In *A Fragment of Life* Machen tries to convince us of a hidden reality.

Taboo, Magic, Spirits
A study of primitive elements in Roman religion
by Eli Edward Burriss
200 pages, Paperback, ISBN 9789492355034

In Ancient Rome Mana was the term used for a mysterious, magical medium, which could be helpful or harmful (Taboo). Just like the Chinese qi, it could empower the positive and the negative. Contents: Mana, Magic and Animism – Positive and Negative Mana (Taboo) – Miscellaneous Taboos – Magic Acts: The General Principles – Removing Evils by - Magic Acts – Incantation and Prayer– Naturalism and Animism.

Chaldean Magic
It's Origin and Development
by François Lenormant
454 pages, Paperback, ISBN 9789492355027

The essentials of magic in Chaldea are presented inside a context of comparison or contrast to Egyptian, Median, Turanian, Finno-Tartarian and Akkadian magic, mythologies, religion and speech. Interesting is the Chaldean demonology, with its incubus, succubus, vampire, nightmare and many Elemental spirits, most of them coalesced with the primal powers of nature.

Amazons - Two publications in one book -
I. *The Amazons* by Guy Cadogan Rothery
II. *Religious Cults Associated With the Amazons*
   by Florence Mary Bennett
328 pages, Paperback, ISBN 9789492355089

Contents I: The Amazons of Antiquity – Amazons in Far Asia – Modern Amazons of the Caucasus – Amazons of Europe – Amazons of Africa – Amazons of America – The Amazon Stones. Contents II: The Amazons in Greek legend – The Great Mother – Ephesian Artemis – Artemis Astrateia and Apollo Amazonius – Ares.